Practicing Imperfection

Practicing Imperfection

A Priest's Journey through Meditation, Messing Up, and Ministry

Charles T. Dupree

Foreword by Curtis Almquist

RESOURCE *Publications* · Eugene, Oregon

PRACTICING IMPERFECTION
A Priest's Journey through Meditation, Messing Up, and Ministry

Resource Publications
An Imprint of Wipf and Stock Publishers
199 W. 8th Ave., Suite 3
Eugene, OR 97401

www.wipfandstock.com

PAPERBACK ISBN: 978-1-4982-9870-4
HARDCOVER ISBN: 978-1-4982-5741-1
EBOOK ISBN: 978-1-4982-9871-1

Manufactured in the U.S.A.   NOVEMBER 21, 2016

Contents

Foreword

THE ANCIENT ETYMOLOGY FOR the English verb "to meditate" is to measure, limit, consider, advise. To meditate is a thoughtful and wise practice. The words "meditate" and "medicine" share the same Latin root, so to meditate is also about the healing and wellness of the soul. To meditate is to breathe in what is life-giving, and to breathe out what is life-clogging or life-compromising. To meditate is respiratory therapy for the soul. To meditate is a salubrious alternative to anesthetizing ourselves with drugs, to habitually escaping through entertainment, to endlessly striving not to disappoint anyone, especially ourselves.

To meditate is to live life intentionally, to engage life responsively not just reactively, to be really present to the gift of now. With all our technology gadgets, it is so easy, so tempting, to be *virtually* present across all kinds of platforms, but not to be *really* present anywhere at all. You can literally gain the whole world with a click on a keyboard, but lose or misplace your soul.

Meditation for the soul is like grammar, punctuation, and syntax to language. Without this ordering, and without space between the words, life becomes like a run-on sentence. It's gibberish. It will make no sense. Meditation for the soul is also like the rests in music. Without the rests—the changes in cadence, the pauses and silences, the primed expectations—what wants to be harmonized, orchestrated, and resolved is just a cacophony of noise.

A practice of meditation is especially important and particularly hard for those involved with the leadership in the church. I'm speaking here of aspirants to Holy Orders, seminarians, and the ordained. I'm also speaking of those who have relationships with these people: family members, colleagues, friends, and parishioners. Most everyone. Meditation is especially hard and particularly important because of the hyper pace of modern-day life, the tyranny of others' urgent expectations, and our own drivenness. Leadership often exposes us at our best *and* at our worst. I was speaking to a Brother in the monastery where I live about some inner conflict I was experiencing. I said to him as an aside, "I guess I've got some 'baggage' around this." My Brother responded, "Curtis, that's not baggage, that's freight!" Our baggage, our freight, needs to be off-loaded and sorted; meditation is such a helpful vehicle for lightening and enlightening our load.

In the Gospel according to Matthew, we hear Jesus say, "Be perfect, as your heavenly Father is perfect. . . ." This may seem both seductive and impossible. In actuality, we're rescued by this word "perfect." In the Greek, this is not a command but rather a promise. In the Greek, this is future tense, not imperative tense. In the end, we will be made perfect, complete, and whole. Jesus promises it will be so. But this conversion is a lifetime process. The founder of my monastic community, Richard Meux Benson, reminds us Jesus' work of perfection in us is gradual. Benson says, "We cannot bound into the depths of God at one spring; if we could we should be shattered, not filled. God draws us on." We're reminded that God has all the time in the world for us—this world, and the next.

In the meantime—and sometimes it is a very mean time— we live with imperfection, which some days can be quite disordered. St. Paul says to "work out your own salvation with fear and trembling." I understand the "work out"; however my emotional repertoire in the workout is much more messy than just "fear and trembling." When I'm reminded again (and again) that I am not my own god, that the end in life is not to get my own way, that other people are trying (or not trying) as hard as I am to pull off life, I get in touch with all kinds of emotions: anger, resistance to surrendering, denial, resentment, despair, humiliation. I have come so far; I have so far to go. The story is told from the early centuries of the church where Christian monasticism was born in the Egyptian desert. An old woman, who had lived her entire life since childhood on the outskirts of a monastery, had one question she had always wanted to ask a monk. But this was an enclosed monastery, the monks never coming outside the monastery precinct. Never. Except one day. One day an old monk came out to walk into the desert. The old woman hobbled toward him to ask him her question of a lifetime: "What do you do in there?" So the story goes, the old monk looked to the ground, then looked to the heavens and, with tears in his eyes, said, "We fall down and we get up again. We fall down and we get up again. We fall down and we get up again." In the stories that follow, Charlie Dupree speaks plenty about falling. I think you will find his transparency inviting, disarming, helpful, hopeful, delightful. I certainly do.

You will also discover that Charlie makes a distinction between meditative practice and prayer. Charlie prays; however this is not a prayer book. For Charlie, meditation is an attentiveness to our own inner voices, thoughts, feelings, and patterns. I find this encouraging. At those moments when my prayer has dried up and when God seems very distant or illusive, I meanwhile have myself. God has entrusted me with myself. Paying attention to what is going on within my own soul will inevitably help me locate God. Or rather, paying attention to what is going on within my own soul will help me discover where and how and why God has found me.

For those who are leaders in the church—and for those who know and relate to them—life is full of challenge and, I would say, equally full of provision. Claiming practices that are life-sustaining is essential. We cannot just be dispensers of help and hope. We need to live the good news of Jesus that we proclaim. You are worth living the abundant life that Jesus promises. Bernard of Clairvaux, the great twelfth-century French abbot, clearly knew about crowds and people with overwhelming needs in his own day. Bernard had a strong admonition particularly for leaders of the church, but, for that matter, what he says can be applied to anyone with eyes to see and a heart to care for the needs of the world that surrounds us. The endless needs. Saint Bernard says that if you are wise, you will be more like a reservoir than a canal. A water canal, he says, spreads abroad the water as it receives it. A canal is a "pass through." A reservoir, on the other hand, waits until it is filled before overflowing. A reservoir, without loss to itself, shares its superabundant water. "In the church at the present day"—this is Bernard speaking about twelfth-century Europe but it is equally true for us today—"we have many canals but few reservoirs." Be a reservoir. You are worth it.

Curtis Almquist, SSJE
Cambridge, Massachusetts

Preface

I DON'T KNOW WHY I started meditating. Three years ago, something just clicked. Maybe it was God who finally helped me name what was going on within me. Maybe I knew my role as an Episcopal priest would kill me and my marriage if I didn't change something. I'm not sure when, but at some point, I was finally able to identify what needed to change: I was tired of worrying, tired of trying to read everyone's mind, and tired of revving the engine. I acknowledged that I couldn't possibly meet everyone's needs and resolved to deal with it. I wanted to be calmer, more clear-minded, and gentler with myself and others.

Trust me, it wasn't easy to set aside twenty to forty minutes every day to sit. It takes practice. The practice of meditation is about putting yourself in the position of learning something new about yourself. The stories in this book are about a new chapter in my life, a chapter strongly influenced and supported by a meditation practice that helps me manage the blessed reality that I am not perfect and that imperfection can, with practice, be a good teacher and the bearer of holiness.

Some disciplines have perfection as a goal. My meditation practice does not. In addition to embracing imperfection, the goal of my meditation practice is to learn how to live a life that is calm, flexible, and filled with good humor, a life that has space for meaningful relationships and interests. None of these things require perfection. Who's ever heard of a perfect relationship or a perfect state of calm and flexibility? Such endeavors involve trying, sometimes failing, and trying again. Meditation should be approached with some degree of interest and curiosity; a measure of compassion, gentleness, and patience is required. And, I believe, love is required—love for ourselves and for others. Meditation is teaching me these things. Meditation is to the mind what exercise is to the body. It is a way of keeping our awareness and our perceptions healthy and vibrant. As the body is made healthier by the practice of exercise, so the mind is made healthier when cobwebs are cleared and layers of dust are blown away. Ultimately, when we practice how to be calmer and more clear-minded, we create a larger space in which to develop healthier, holier connections to the beauty and mysteries of life. Some might call this prayer.

As a priest, I have often thought and been told that the practice of meditation is equivalent to prayer. At this point in my life, I maintain a separate practice for each. I have a prayer life in which I listen for clarity and for God's direction concerning how to move through life. I also have a meditation life in which I am attentive to my own inner voices, thoughts, feelings, and patterns. Having two different practices is helpful. Every now and then, though, they merge into something that is entirely "other." I don't know what is being born at those times, but I hope it is my truer self. As Thomas Merton once wrote, "The quest for the true self is part of the quest to let God know you as you are."[1] I am on a quest to know who I am, and I trust the journey is making me truer to the person God made me to be and intended me to become.

Even as a priest, I don't have all the answers. I struggle with how to live a good, balanced life. I struggle with my ego; I'm jealous of those more fortunate and successful than I, all because I still wrestle with that thing called "perfection." I guess there are some areas of life where perfection is achievable, but in my line of work, perfection won't happen until another time and space. For now, then, I have to learn how to manage and reframe my imperfection.

1. Martin James, *Becoming Who You Are: Insights on the True Self from Thomas Merton and Other Saints* (Mahwah, NJ: Paulist, 2006), 28.

Usually, when we say we've changed our minds, it means we've changed our opinion on a subject. "I used to think this way, but I changed my mind." As a result of meditation practice, my mind has changed not on any particular subject, but in terms of my general approach to the situations of life.

Life is busy. It doesn't like to create time for practice. But something—a three-month sabbatical—recently came my way that allowed me to recharge my spiritual and personal batteries. During this sabbatical, I put down some thoughts about how meditation intersects with my spiritual and personal life. The stories that follow describe how I understand what it means to be a religious person, a spiritual person, a normal person, a not-so-perfect person. They tell how, on my better days, I have learned not to beat myself up for not getting everything right. And they tell how the practice of meditating every day (well, almost every day) for four years has helped me change my mind.

Acknowledgments

I OWE THANKS TO all of those mentioned in this book. You are important to me. In addition, I want to thank a few people behind the words and pages:

Gray Lesesne, Andy Kort, Mihee Kim-Kort, Janette Fishell, Samantha Ezzo, Michael Fox, Darrell and Katie Case. You have supported me in this process. You help me remember myself, have fun, and laugh.

The congregations I've served. You are gracious and caring and have helped me grow. Each of you has taught me something important about myself and about God.

Suzy. You are my teacher and guide.

The Lily Endowment Clergy Renewal Program. Your generous grant made my sabbatical a possibility.

Matthew. You, more than anyone, know my imperfections and you love me anyway. Thank you.

1

Breath

"ARE YOU AWAKE?" ASKED Jake.

"Yes," I responded.

"—because a lot of people fall asleep in there," he said.

I was listening to Jake, the MRI technician, through a headset. An MRI is not a prerequisite for sabbatical—I was just getting it out of the way so I wouldn't have to worry about it while I was gone. My doctor had decided he wanted to take a look at my bile ducts. An MRI would afford him a look at that which God knit and that which only God, ordinarily, should see.

"Fall asleep? No way! How could that be?" I asked.

Jake responded that the ticking, buzzing rhythms of the machine often lulled people into a deep sleep. And for those who didn't find the experience hypnotic, he said, medication was prescribed to keep them relaxed inside this coffin-like chamber. I did not receive said medication, as tight quarters aren't a problem for me.

We came to a point in the test that focused on my spleen. Since the spleen rests under the diaphragm, the clearest shot for the camera is at the end of an inhalation, when the diaphragm is lifted. Jake offered instructions through the headphones: "Charles, this next part is going to last six minutes. I need you to just breathe nice and steady. But don't go to sleep."

"Roger that. Will do." The ticking and humming began all around me. I thought I'd use the time to enter my meditative zone and employ my steadiest breathing in order to stay centered and calm and get as much out of the moment as possible. After a lot of ticking and buzzing, Jake came through the headset: "Charles, are you awake?"

"Yessir."

Silence.

"I'm just going to reset the machine. Something didn't work right."

"Okeydokey."

The same whirring and buzzing started, and I drew upon my practice of breathing deeply, steadily, and with intentional observation.

"Charles, are you asleep?"

"I'm awake," I said.

"Um," he continued, "are you breathing?"

"Yes," I said in a puzzled tone.

"OK, let's try this again. Remember. Keep your breathing nice and steady."

I went back to my breathing practice, watching the breath as it came in and went out. After more repetitions of ticking and buzzing, and for a period clearly longer than six minutes, a perturbed Jake came through the loudspeaker.

"Charles, stay awake for me."

"I'm awake!"

I then heard the door to the control booth open. I emerged from the tube, feet first, on a narrow table. When I could once again see the ceiling, Jake came into view. Arms crossed over his chest, he looked like a third-grade teacher prepared to scold me.

"We need to talk," he said.

"Why? What? What's going on?"

"We need to talk about your breathing?"

"Why? I'm an excellent breather. What's the problem?"

"Well," Jake explained, "your breathing is so slow that the camera can't stay fixed on your diaphragm and the machine keeps cutting off—this could take hours! I need you to keep your breathing nice and steady."

I was beginning to understand the issue. I asked him to demonstrate what he meant by nice and steady. Jake breathed in and out, but his breathing was neither nice nor steady—it was as though he had just finished a long run. Trying my best to contain my frustration and curb my annoying obsession with proving I am right, I said, "Jake. We all have different interpretations of what 'nice and steady breathing' means." He wasn't impressed.

We were nearing the end of the hour allotted for my twenty-minute test, so Jake, trying to contain *his* frustration, very clearly said to me, "OK. Whatever. But that's the way I need you to breathe; otherwise this test won't work and you'll have to come back later."

Got it. Back into the tube I went.

***

A book about meditation should begin with the breath, for breathing is at the beginning of it all. In the medical dramas of my 1970s childhood, the smug male doctor always gives the fragile newborn a swat on the behind. Why? To make it breathe. Although I'm sure this practice is now forbidden and blamed for contributing to the problems of a violent world, it does prove a point. The breath is important.

Breathing lies at the center of meditation. If meditation were basketball, breathing would be free throws; always practice your free throws. If meditation were practicing an instrument, breathing would be practicing scales. The breath is the foundation upon which meditation practice is built and from which all insight and growth happens.

If I had to guess why the breath is so central to meditation, I would say it is because the breath is always with us. No matter what happens to us, we always have our breath. No matter what circumstances we face, we always have our breath to bring us back to reality. Our breath is a constant reminder that we are alive, that we have spirit, that we have life force. The breath also tells us if we are anxious, worried, scared, tense. When we stop to observe our breathing, we can check our spiritual, physical, and emotional temperature. When we pay attention to it, we are more present and more aware of what is going on. When we fail to pay attention to it, we rush through the day without being aware of what is happening around us and within us.

Why is the breath central? Each breath is different. And like each moment, each breath comes and then goes. The breath, therefore, reminds us to accept and to let go. We accept that which comes to us, noticing it for what it is, and then we let it go. Breathing is a built-in reminder that our lives are filled with things that come and things that go. And each breath, like each moment, gives us what we need—life.

The word *genesis* shares its root with the English words *gene* and *genetics* and *genus*. They all have to do with being born. In the biblical book of Genesis, which is the ancient Jewish tradition's first account of divine–human relations, the author tries to make sense of how life has come into being. "In the beginning," it famously starts—"In the beginning when God created the heavens and the earth, the earth was a formless void and darkness covered the face of the deep, while a wind from God swept over the face of the waters."[1] This word *wind* translates the Hebrew *ruach*. *Ruach* can be translated also as *spirit* or *breath*. These ancient, multiple meanings hold great importance for us. Why is breathing so important in meditation? Because the breath is at the center of our birth. It reminds us that we are born from the same stuff as the rest of the world. Our breath keeps us connected to the other things that occupied the Creator's imagination—the waters of the sea, the stars of the heavens, birds, even the creepy-crawly things. We shared the womb with these things. Our breath reminds us that we share the gift of being created and being creative. We are not alone as we move through life. We share connective tissue with all that has life, light, and breath.

Why is the breath at the center of meditation? Because meditation begins and ends with our aliveness. Meditation is about cultivating a heart that is open and aware and eager to be comfortable with all life has to offer. This can happen at any place, in any moment, even at 7:00 a.m. in a hospital. Even there, even then, we

1. Gen 1:1–2 (NRSV).

can find our breath and come to a place of stasis—an awareness of the holiness of all life.

***

As it turns out, meditating inside an MRI machine doesn't get the job done. With a clearer set of breathing instructions from the technician, I reentered the tube.

"You ready, Charles?"

"I'm ready, Jake."

This time, I breathed my ass off. I did not fall asleep. I stayed awake. Wasn't that the point? To stay awake?

Amidst the whirs and buzzes of magnets, gears, and who knows what else that stirred around me, I was awake and thankful. I was thankful for the blessings of health insurance, medical technology, and skilled physicians and healers. I was awestruck to be inside a machine that took pictures of my insides. I was awake to my connection with the stars of heaven and the birds of the air and awake to the wonder and mystery of life.

"Are you awake?" Jake, my Buddha for the day, had asked as we began our morning together.

What an important question.

2

Surfing

I'VE NEVER UNDERSTOOD SURFING. There's not a lot of juice for the squeeze. Even though I know next to nothing about surfing or surfboards, there I was, watching surfers on a beach in Encinitas, California, one of the top surfing destinations in the country. As luck, or the Spirit, or the universe would have it, this lovely place happened to be the first stop on my sabbatical journey. I had no way of knowing if these surfers were any good. All I knew was there were waves and there were surfers. The waves of my imagination flowed straight from the opening credits of *Hawaii Five-O*. Although the actual waves before me weren't that big, they seemed big enough for the surfers to do their thing. The best thing about them was their hair. From the fashion perspective, I totally got it. Still, it seemed like surfing itself involved a lot of effort only to spend a few seconds actually riding the wave.

Suddenly, my eye caught someone zipping across the crest of a wave. He rode its edge for a good ten seconds, which seemed like a long time to me. The wave underneath him dissolved. He hopped off his board, caught it under his arm, and shook the salt water from his fabulous hair. I watched him as he turned and pushed his way out beyond the breakers, readying himself for another wave. "OK," I thought, "maybe there's more to surfing than meets the lazy eye."

I took a deep breath and kept watching. He bobbed up and down, moving with the rhythm of the water. I tried to tune in to his surfer's, Zen mind:

"Here comes one! Go for it!"
Buddha say: Nope, not the right time.

"Dang! That was a good one, and it got away!"
Buddha say: No worries, another one will come along.

"Shit! There went the most perfect wave ever!"
Buddha say: Chill, brother. Every wave is perfect.

"I'll never get the hang of this."
Buddha say: Nothing is permanent. Tomorrow will be different.

Of course, I projected many of my own patterns of thinking onto this innocent surfer. I prayed, though, that he wasn't thinking as much as I was. Meditation teaches us to live not in the past or in the future, but in the moment. As I stared into the waves, I realized this might be why surfers are so utterly relaxed. The waves call us to stop thinking. They represent observation, patience, and presence. When we stop thinking, all the elements of action come together in that perfect combination of effort and effortlessness.

Back to the surfer. Heart and mind cooperating, he was up again before he knew it. He cut a long line parallel to the shore. Although his feet were planted firmly on the fiberglass board, his body was as fluid as the water underneath him. True, the ride lasted only ten seconds, but something about it seemed perfect. For those ten seconds, he glided on the edge of the continent, drawn from point A to point B by something other than himself.

Maybe this is the point of surfing. Don't we all want to be carried along by something that is not ourselves? We spend so much time paddling, struggling, and forcing square pegs into round holes. We spend so much time pushing against the current. We beat ourselves up if we don't catch every single wave. We push ourselves into the crazy-making belief that every wave is ours for the taking and if we don't take it, we've missed the opportunity of a lifetime. Perhaps success in surfing lies in the acceptance that the waves don't belong to us. They are a gift. Surfing, and all of life, is about skillfully and patiently connecting with the Spirit's current—watching, waiting, and in the right moment, making the decision to act. We keep our elbows, hips, and knees slightly bent so that we can flex with the energy that moves underneath us. This takes practice.

But do I want to practice this hard? Maybe this is why, when I watch surfers, I get exhausted. Do I want to dangle my legs in the water and imagine sharks beneath me? Do I want to get all that sand in my shorts and water up my nose? Do I want to put myself through falling over and over again?

We all practice something. The trick is to be aware of what we're practicing; otherwise, we might overlook what it teaches us. We might overlook that we have moved from point A to point B, that we have made progress. By waves or wings or something else, we have been carried toward a newer, needed shore.

Surfing. Do I give myself to surfing?

I'm old enough now to realize I can't take on another great endeavor, but I can stop and consider what surfing has to teach me about my life. I can stop and pay attention to the waves of experience that call upon my intuition, my timing, my patience. I can practice falling. I can practice getting up. I can practice looking like a victor. I can practice looking like a fool. I can practice frustration. I can practice calm. I can practice.

Each of us has something like surfing in our life, something that demands the same kind of practiced balance. Each of us has something we have given our heart to, something that takes us from point A to point B on a razor's edge of effort and effortlessness. And yes, we have to practice not only the technical skills of our craft, but also the balance it takes to stay upright, even if we fall embarrassingly on our heads. I fall plenty, and will continue to do so. Thanks to a lot of practice, I'm better at falling than I once was. I have moved from point A to point B, and hopefully, points C and D are out there somewhere.

In the meantime, closer to shore, a little boy practiced on a smaller board. In water up to his knees, he threw himself into every wave that came his way. He already knew what it was like to be taken by another agency from point A to point wherever. And he was addicted. Good luck, young surfer, and try not to forget this feeling. Maybe, one day, you'll find yourself on this same beach. Maybe you'll be out there in a wet suit with fabulous hair riding those large breakers. Or maybe, like me, you will be in a beach chair, watching, celebrating, and gleaning insight into the mysteries of life.

Whichever way the waves take you, enjoy the journey, and at day's end, however you get there, give praise and thanks to the Spirit of life that is always taking you where you need to go.

3

Sunset

One day tells its tale to another.

PSALM 19

I'D NEVER SEEN A proper sunset. Sure, I'd seen the sun *go down*. I'd seen the sun go down over the fields of my farm in North Carolina. I'd seen the sun descend over the sound on the Outer Banks. I'd seen the sun go down over the blue grasses of Kentucky. But a sunset? A one-word *sunset*? There's a big difference between a sunset and the action of the sun's descent. I'd just seen a sunset for the first time—over the Pacific Ocean. This was the first time I'd watched the sun do its thing over an unobstructed expanse of space. Nothing between it and me, the sun dropped, simply, quietly, into the water. Not until this moment had the psalmist's phrase made sense to me:

One day tells its tale to another.

The phrase is strange. But then again, most scholars believe it was written approximately 2,500 years ago. This particular psalm speaks about God's law. As the sun gives light, so the law of God gives light and insight. Even though the author (a poet) was filled with insight, she or he didn't know how the sun worked.

This ancient artist had no idea where the sun went when it could no longer be seen. So the poet stared and thought and stared and thought some more. One day, inspired by the light of the law of the Lord, the psalmist crafted some lines that evoked a setting sun. After seeing this activity time and time again, the poet captured the repetitiveness of discipline and the discipline of repetitiveness—one day tells its tale to another.

There I sat, thousands of years later, on the Pacific Coast. I dug a bit deeper. Following the psalmist's musings, I asked myself, "How can a day say anything? Why would one day want to talk to another day, and what would it want to say?" The image of two women came to mind.

They are neighbors. Their families have grown up eating at each other's dinner tables. Each wife has permission to discipline the other's kids and yell at the other's spouse. They are closer than sisters. They are important women who have tended to important matters. Day after day, they have sent their children off to school or work. They have stood behind their husbands or wives, encouraging them, day after day, to return to jobs they hate. "Just stick it out another day," they might say to their spouses, whose patience has been stretched thin by an asshole boss or an unfair salary. These women have done the laundry, cooked the meals, mended the socks and the underwear. They have canned the tomatoes and creamed the corn. In other words, these women have kept the heartbeat of their families strong and steady. Finally, as always, they carve out a space to breathe. At the end of the day, with a shot of something or other in their glasses, they meet. To each other, and to each other only, they share the details of their day. They let the other know what they have seen, what they have thought, what they have imagined. They tell each other the secrets of the household, trusting that the information will remain within the intimate circuit of their friendship. They tell each other about the course of another typical day, saluting each other for their hard work, their loyalty, and the strength it takes to lay their egos aside for the good of the cause. Each tells her tale to the other.

As the sun set over the Pacific, I could almost hear one day telling its tale to the next. I could almost hear one day recount that, now as always, people were born and people died. There was war making. There was peacemaking. Music was made. Love was made. Technology that will heal was created, as was technology that will destroy. Some will go to bed hungry, some with hope in their hearts. "This is what I've seen," one day says to the next. "It's nothing I haven't seen before."

Receiving the information with a quiet smile, the next day awakens. With any luck, the information can be used to make the new day different, better, more peaceful. With any luck, the new day's tale will not include hunger, war, suicide, negligence, anger, hate. With any luck. With any luck.

Meditation practice allows us to pay attention to the beginning and end of each breath. We are invited to be curious about how one breath is different from the next. We are invited to be aware of how each inhalation gives way to an exhalation. In that tiny space between them, there is peace. This is the space occupied by those two brave ladies with their glasses of "job well done." They revel in the peace of what they've accomplished and the space they've created for themselves—for the world. One day passes the baton to another and says, "Here. See what you can do with this one. There's still plenty of good yet to be born."

Opportunity. Resurrection. Birth. Renewal. Faith. Strength.

This is what I saw when I experienced my first sunset. One day exhaled. Another day inhaled. Our sunset turned into someone else's sunrise. The hard work of one day, I continue to believe, will inform a new day somewhere else. Like two fierce ladies—like generations upon generations of fierce ladies—we keep showing up, tending to our families, tending to our friends, doing what we are called to do. We breathe in. We breathe out. We pray. We are prayed for. We progress. We regress. Doesn't matter. The important part is that we are a part of the tale.

We pass our sunsets, one to the other, until one day—one fine day—we all get it right.

4

Yoga and Weight Lifting

PLACING A YOGA STUDIO beside a weight-training facility seems like a bad idea. I'm sure a feng shui book somewhere would agree.

Yoga is all about being in touch with your breath. Through postures (asanas), we move and flow, always maintaining awareness of our breath. These postures can be challenging (you've seen the magazine covers). Even though people like me can't come close to touching their noses to their knees, these postures awaken us to our physicality and can make us huff and puff. The goal of yoga, however, is not to huff and puff. With the help of an instructor, we may choose to adjust the physical postures in such a way as to keep our breathing steady and regular. If we are huffing and puffing, we're pushing too hard and could hurt ourselves.

A major teaching in yoga is *ahimsa*. The Sanskrit word means "do no violence," and the concept includes not only the violence we may inflict on others, but also the violence we may inflict on ourselves. In yoga, we are called not to injure ourselves in body, mind, or spirit. We practice yoga to take care of ourselves. Knowing the limits of our hamstrings and spines, we know what we need from the experience, and we know what might bring about unproductive suffering. Based on our particular need or state of mind, we set an intention at the beginning of our practice that keeps us focused and grounded. Perhaps we need to be gentle with ourselves today. Perhaps we want to be more flexible in the hips. Perhaps we want to be more flexible in our attitude toward our neighbor. Maybe we want to listen closely to the calmer, more reasonable parts of our mind. The intention is up to the individual practitioner.

For me, the intention always has to do with staying on the mat. This is another way of saying "leave your ego at the door." This is a constant battle for me. My ego and I are inseparable. But my yoga practice is an opportunity to leave it behind.

If I stay on the mat, I'm there only with myself. But if I mentally leave the mat, I can't help but compare myself to the guy or gal on the three-by-six-foot piece of real estate next door. We try not to compare ourselves to the person beside us—who clearly works for Cirque du Soleil as a contortionist. Staying on the mat means I do not try to outdo the people around me. It means staying in my own space, exploring my own opportunities for growth, and keeping my focus in the here and now.

So, knowing me (and my ego) the way I know me (and my ego), why in God's name would I practice yoga beside a weight-lifting facility? Outside, men and women *were* huffing and puffing. They were dropping weights. They were shouting at each other: "Harder!" "Faster!" "More!" A timer was on, and the trainer counted down emphatically: "Five, four, three, two, one—go!" Everything happening around me, including the workouts of the chiseled, Greek-like twenty-five-year-olds, was trying to pull me away from what was happening on my mat.

But as I lay on my back in a final, calming pose called *shav-asana*—as I tried to integrate everything I'd done, thought, and felt while a rapper's song blasted through the loudspeakers—a gentle smile rolled across my lips and, with it, a light bulb: unless we do something about it, noise will always drown out quiet and push us into unhealthy territory.

By design, loudness has to rise above the sounds in its environment. We are loud when we are in danger, when we are in pain. Animals are loud when they want to establish their turf or want a partner to notice them. Alarms and whistles are loud to keep our stuff and us safe. Ships' horns and trains' whistles are loud so others can get out of their way. Things are loud to get our attention. Loudness can serve our planet and us. But loudness can also distract.

Unless we train our hearts and minds, we might think loudness is the only alternative. There are other voices, though. There are voices of space, length, calm, stillness, joy—and each of us has these voices. They are strong, but they are quiet. They are easily overtaken. They are wise voices, but they are also patient—they wait.

"You'll hear us when you're ready," they say. "We're not going to shout."

We have to create the space where we can hear them. We need people to coach or teach us, to guide us onto paths of opportunity and health. The teacher's voice might even be loud—from time to time, a teacher may need to shout. But we have some control over which of the loud voices we honor. Are they skilled voices? Are they supportive? Do they challenge us in ways that bring about our best qualities? And do they bring us to places of discovery and fullness of life? If not, they're just noise we need to tune out. A variety of voices is helpful, but we have to be careful not to listen only to the loud ones. It's easy to listen to the loud ones—they are familiar. It's not so easy to listen to the quiet voices. So, we practice.

We practice listening to the quiet ones, the quiet voices we hear only when we're listening specifically for them. I am reminded of the character Mary, who sat at Jesus's feet when he visited her house.[1] Mary's sister, Martha, set about readying the house for her guest. Luke's Jesus uses the Greek word *perispaomai*, which means "distracted." According to one scholar, the Greek term is used only once in the New Testament and literally means "pulled in many directions."[2] Martha, understandably, was pulled by the many voices that told her to conform to the traditional patterns of behavior for women of that time and culture. But Mary listened to a different voice. Mary made the decision to put herself into a space of listening in which she was able to hear a voice that might otherwise remain concealed. It also strikes me that Mary listened

---

1. Luke 10:38–42.
2. Stoffregen, "Exegetical note on Luke 10:38–42," line 45.

to the voice that was present—not to the voices of the future or the past, but to the voice that was before her in that moment.

In this competitive, complicated world, the louder voices are overwhelming, especially the voices of the past and the future. They are the voices of "I wish I had done things differently" or "I'd better be prepared for everything!" They are regret and fear. They keep us up at night. They are powerful.

But every now and then, the quiet voice of the moment sneaks in and speaks a more gentle truth. Therefore, we must create space for it and give it a chance to speak. We quiet our bodies—as well as our spirits and minds—in order to invite balance into our lives. We may even have to do this work next to noisy, frantic spaces. But these quieter voices are important if we are truly to do no harm to ourselves or others.

Where do you listen to your quiet voices? Whether you listen to them in church, in a yoga studio, at a gym, in a meditation garden, or during your lunch break on a bench somewhere, thank you for creating the space to listen to them, for their only job in life is to serve you and your neighbor. They may not ever shout at you, but their message is loud and clear.

Namaste. Shalom. Amen.

5

Passing the Time

When I was a young boy, I would often visit my grandmother. These visits weren't formal or planned—"Oh, I need to visit my grandmother today." She and my family shared a farm. As a child, I could wander more extensively than the typical nine-year-old. If I got bored (which was often), I would wander through a field of peanuts or soybeans or cotton or tobacco or corn and walk without knocking into grandma's house. She was always there. Unfortunately, at a point much earlier in my childhood, she had a stroke, and she could no longer walk without assistance. She sat in a chair pretty much all day. From that chair, she would watch the day go by. Occasionally, if she felt up to it, she would amble out to her front porch. I would join her there, and this is what I remember whenever I sit outside at a coffee shop enjoying a three-dollar cup of coffee. I think of the evenings we spent on her front porch.

We lived on a fairly major road in Eastern North Carolina that stretched, as my father said, "from Florida to Maine." It wasn't an incredibly busy highway, but it saw a good amount of traffic. Grandma enjoyed making a game out of it. "Choose a color," she'd say. We'd each choose a color, and when a car of that color passed, we'd get a point. So there we sat, watching the cars pass, forgetting about the clock.

Ah, what I wouldn't do for the ability not to keep an eye on the clock.

My therapist and I talk about this frequently. I have a strong internal clock, and I'm always counting off time, constantly multi-tasking. One of the goals of my sabbatical, according to my therapist, was to practice doing nothing. Of course, throughout the sabbatical, I wrote, so I didn't exactly do nothing. I guess it's time to admit it.

My name is Charlie, and I'm addicted to productivity. This is a great addiction for a priest. Congregations always want their priests to be productive. Start a new Bible study, restructure our staff, build our endowment, visit me in the hospital, read the book I put in your mailbox, read the article I slid under the door of your office, preach a good sermon, give me one minute of your time, look at all this stuff other churches are doing—you might want to try some of it! I have created a relationship with a system that will always feed my addiction. I have a lot of ideas, I have a lot of energy, and I like to do new things. Over the course of sixteen years of ministry, I have not stopped reinventing, redeveloping, and reimagining. This means I don't let one minute of time pass that is not under my control. I can turn even a simple, front-porch game with my grandmother into a major undertaking.

Meditation has helped immensely with my addiction to productivity. In fact, each moment of meditation is an antidote to this addiction. In meditation, we neither concern ourselves with the past nor anticipate the future. Thoughts come and go like cars on a busy highway. And we let them go. We let thoughts and time pass, doing nothing. We try not to fill the spaces with our to-do lists.

Behind my addiction is a father who didn't tolerate inactivity. Doing nothing was shameful. If we weren't doing anything, he would put us to work. Like a priest, I guess, farmers always have something to do. Behind my father's addiction was a certain fear of losing crops and income as a result of inactivity. In my family, the importance of standing *en garde*, and of appearing busy even when we weren't, was always emphasized.

I suppose I've transformed my entire congregation of three or four hundred people into a huge family of father figures. In my mind, they, too, are secretly waiting to catch me doing nothing so they can put me to work.

Lord, have mercy.

I write this for priests who, like me, are addicted to people pleasing and productivity. I sympathize. We make hard work even harder. We layer additional voices that tell us to do more on top of an already difficult and demanding job. God's call to this ministry is real, important, and fulfilling. It also takes discipline. We have to practice hearing God's voice and knowing what it sounds like. We also have to practice knowing what God's voice does not sound like. We have to tune our ears to a voice that is ever-changing but constant, always speaking but silent. God speaks sometimes through wind and thunder, sometimes through the people who bug the shit out of us. Some people are called to cloister themselves from the hustling world in order to focus their attention on God's voice without interruption. We parish priests, though—we have to do it every day in the midst of peoples' pains, problems, and bad moods. Easy, right?

To those congregations who think their priests aren't doing enough: cut them some slack. They're probably more worried about it than you are. You may have the rare lazy priest (they do exist), but your priest is probably engaged in a constant internal dialogue, a push and pull, asking, "Am I getting this right? Am I doing enough?"

And, if your priest is like me, doing nothing is a real challenge. It doesn't come naturally to her or him.

Mercifully, for this part of my sabbatical, God blessed me with a beautiful front porch in a coastal town in Eastern North Carolina. I forced myself to sit on it. After fifteen minutes, I usually began to fidget and twist, grabbing my phone to see if anyone had texted or called. Typically, no one had.

I watched men and women walking their dogs. I watched kids go to school and adults go to work. I thought of my grandmother and watched the cars and trucks pass. A white one. A red one. A silver one. For a moment, I got lost in a good memory that connected to another good memory. For a little while, I found myself doing nothing, and it felt really good.

6

Sacrifice

Assisi, Italy—Part I

ASSISI IS THE HOME of one of the most famous saints in the world—
St. Francis. Among those familiar with him, he is most commonly
known as the patron saint of animals, largely because he honored
them and humanity's need for them. He is believed to have given
extra portions of food to livestock and birds on Christmas Eve. He
also knew, ahead of his time, that even the smallest of creatures in
the system of life deserve our respect and protection. Francis was a
pioneer ecologically and spiritually, but this wasn't always the case.
All records indicate that in his teens, Francis was a directionless
punk. His parents didn't make things much better. They gave him
whatever he needed to continue his life of frivolity. Francis wasn't
his given name; it was John. His mother named him after John the
Baptist, but his dad didn't want his son to be named after a crazy
vagrant. So Dad gave him the name Francis because of his love of
France, a place to which father and son traveled often.

While he didn't quite know what to do with his life, Francis
could dream. His dream was to become a famous knight. In his
attempt to do so, he took part in a civil skirmish in Assisi that
got him captured and imprisoned. During his imprisonment, he
became frail and thin and contracted malaria, a disease that stayed

with him the rest of his life. His parents paid off Francis's captors, and Francis returned to his normal life with the folks. After a full year of recovery, Francis resumed his work with his father in the fabric business. One hot summer afternoon, Francis was running an errand at one of his father's properties, about a mile outside of town. To escape the heat and take a break (and enjoy a nap, perhaps), Francis entered an old, neglected church called San Damiano. There, God spoke to him from a cross. "Restore my Church," God said. At last, a purpose, a vision, a mission, a direction in life. Francis started a movement that would make an enduring mark on Christianity. Under his leadership, this movement would call the Church back to its original mission—to care for the poor, and to lay aside all that distracts us from loving God and neighbor.[1]

One of my goals during sabbatical was to visit Assisi. I wanted to see the homeland of St. Francis. For a priest, looking deeply into the life of Francis is deeply humbling. Francis, after all, dropped everything and tended to those around him who were sick and suffering. He even lived on a leper colony. I began to wonder about what I had really given up in order to follow God's call. I hadn't abandoned my wealth. I hadn't given up physical pleasures. I struggle all the time with setting proper boundaries, boundaries that keep me healthy and sane. Francis might have said, "Screw boundaries! Do anything and everything for the sake of Christ."

I began to think about this. In becoming a priest, had I made, do I make, any sacrifices?

In preparing for my time away, I tried hard to create the space that would allow me to really unplug. I would not receive calls from parishioners. I would not attend to parish minutiae. I would not respond to a million questions about committees and policies and timelines. The space I created would be free of anxiety, worry, and guilt. Getting away from parish life would rid me of worldly cares.

Sure it would.

A common misconception about meditation practice is that it is supposed to kill all thought—that it will create a mind that

---

1. Details of the life of St. Francis are taken from Donald Spoto, *Reluctant Saint: The Life of Francis of Assisi* (New York: Penguin, 2002).

is blank, a white canvas free of activity. But this is not the goal of meditation. When we sit, we observe the thoughts that come and go. We watch them, acknowledge their presence, and let them go. The brain is designed to work around the clock. Even at night, it doesn't turn off. It continues to generate thoughts and fills our heads with a crazy soup of memories and images. We can't stop thoughts, but we can train our minds to respond to them differently. We can train our minds to be more focused, less congested, and clearer.

I had imagined that during sabbatical, all of life around me would stop. But just as we can't keep thoughts from entering our minds, we can't force life to stop happening. While I was on sabbatical, life continued to change in its unpredictable way: I worried about whether I had made bad decisions. I had anxiety about relationships. I felt guilty about being away from my congregation for so long. A friend's brother died; another friend's brother tragically completed a suicide attempt. A family friend invited me to officiate at her wedding. My mother fell in the bathroom twice. Visits to family were no less dysfunctional and stressful than before. Making plans to see friends stirred up the same scheduling stress I always experience. And, to top it off, someone hacked and charged $8,000 to my helpless credit card. Even as I tried to unplug, the world continued to reach out to me. I responded as brother, as son, as husband, as friend, as mentor, as rector, as priest.

In case you're wondering what we priests "agree" to, the following is an excerpt from "The Examination," a part of the ordination ceremony of the Episcopal Church:

> As a priest, it will be your task to proclaim by word and deed the Gospel of Jesus Christ, and to fashion your life in accordance with its precepts. You are to love and serve the people among whom you work, caring alike for young and old, strong and weak, rich and poor. You are to preach, to declare God's forgiveness to penitent sinners, to pronounce God's blessing, to share in the administration of Holy Baptism and in the celebration of the mysteries of Christ's Body and Blood, and to perform the other ministrations entrusted to you.

In all that you do, you are to nourish Christ's people from the riches of his grace, and strengthen them to glorify God in this life and in the life to come.[2]

In all that I do . . .

Did I make sacrifices in becoming a priest? Well, not to the extent that Francis did (he was never ordained, by the way). The big realization for me was that I sacrificed the option of being anything other than a priest. As a priest, I am unable to detach from my deeply held conviction that I should take up the caring concerns of Christ. In other words, I am and will always be a priest. I have taken on this way of life, and no matter how hard I try, I can't stop being a priest. I can take the phone off the hook and I can stop checking e-mails, but I will always be priest. Sometimes this is a great honor and joy, and sometimes it is a great burden that causes me to question, even resent, the way I am called to live my life.

The sacrifice of my life isn't about what I've "given up." It's about my decision to respond to God in a particular way. It's about my decision to make the building of God's Church the most important thing in my life. Holiness of life always involves sacrifice.

Compared to Francis and the sacrifices he made, I am a lightweight. I still struggle with my interactions with the homeless and those who are hurting. There are times when I have the strength to meet them head-on. There are times when I'm a spoiled, arrogant coward who crosses the street to avoid their cardboard signs. I guess I'm doing OK if there is still some struggle present. Maybe *that's* the most important ingredient of sacrifice. As long as we're struggling, wrestling with the right thing to do and the right way to be, listening for how God is shaping our way of life, we move toward holiness.

Francis called the Church back to itself. He wouldn't let the Church forget that its center was in the compassionate love of Jesus. Since then, the Church has moved away from and toward this center multiple times. I, too, want the Church to come back to the place Francis identified. I want the Church to be a visible

---

2. *Book of Common Prayer* (New York: Church, 1979), 531.

sign of the love of God and compassion of Jesus. Does the Church, like Francis, need to give up everything, including its buildings, its music, its stodgy, slow way of moving, in order to be a place of reconciliation, learning, and joy—a place of safety? As I once heard somebody say, "The Church is most itself when it is walking away from power and wealth." This would involve a lot of sacrifice on the part of a lot of people, including me. I don't know how I feel about these ideas.

We may not fulfill Francis's vision in my lifetime, but I still hold it before me. I struggle with the tensions involved in this kind of life. I struggle with the voices that push and pull. I try to listen. I pray I will always want to be a priest. For now, I do, but I have to wonder. It's hard work, building up the Church, especially now, when it seems to be losing steam, but that's a different story. So my prayer is that God will empower me to do the ancient work of building the Church. And my prayer is that in building, I will be rebuilt, and that people will see in me an instrument of peace. Perhaps a confused, overactive, anxiety-ridden instrument of peace, but an instrument nonetheless, trying to do God's holy will.

Prayer before the Cross of San Damiano

Most high glorious God,
Pour your light into the darkness of my heart.
Give me right faith, certain hope, and perfect charity,
Sense and knowledge, Lord,
That I may do your holy will.
Amen.

7

Steps

Assisi, Italy—Part II

MY SISTER, SANDY, INTRODUCED me to counting my steps. It's kind of a thing these days. Evidently, a person is supposed to walk a minimum of ten thousand steps each day. According to studies conducted in other countries, where people are skinnier and more fit than in the United States, this is the case because people walk more places: to the grocery store, to the post office, to the end of the street. Keeping track of your steps is one way to encourage yourself to exercise, I suppose. People have all kinds of ways of monitoring the steps they take each day, and I'm not talking about the old-school pedometers you wear on your shoe. This is satellite-based technology! If you go from here to there, a satellite knows it and computes the number of steps it took you to do so.

I have something on my iPhone that counts my steps. I'm not sure whether a satellite does it or a gizmo inside the phone detects when I'm walking or running. At the end of each day, I can take a look at it to see how many steps I've taken, how many miles I've walked, and how many floors I've climbed. It also computes averages of my walking and climbing activity. In Assisi (a city built on the side of a steep hill), I walked a daily average of 12,623 steps, or 5.65 miles. I climbed an average of thirty-eight floors.

There are approximately eight thousand steps between Francis's childhood home and the famous chapel of San Damiano. I walked them. The app on my phone counted them. Even though he walked them many times, Francis wouldn't have known how many steps there were. He also wouldn't have known how many steps there were between Assisi and the Porziuncola, the other local church that he helped restore and that now sits encased in a glorious basilica outside the walls of Assisi. He wouldn't have counted his steps, probably, even if he could have.

As the chair of the diocesan Commission on Ministry, I know there are no less than sixty steps a person must take if she or he wants to be ordained in the Episcopal Church. These steps involve everything from writing a spiritual autobiography to visiting a psychiatrist. Francis wouldn't have counted these steps, either. He was not ordained. He was just a normal person who had no idea that his life would move in this direction. He would never have pointed out to anyone how many steps toward holiness he had taken in his life. He would never have counted how many steps he walked alongside the sick and wounded. He would never have said to the church officials, "Just look at how far I've walked to get here!" He didn't do what he did so others could record his successes. He did what he did because he sought a deeper, truer sense of God. He wanted to show people a real God who was made known in a real world. Jesus was made real in the variety of personalities who followed Francis, and Jesus was made real in the lepers to whom his clan of Brothers and friends attended. As Jesus was of the world, Francis was of the world. Which makes me wonder: Would Francis have wanted to know how many steps Jesus took? From Jerusalem to Galilee? From the Temple to the Pool of Bethzatha? From Levi's house to the house of Lazarus, Mary, and Martha? Would Francis have been interested in knowing how many steps Jesus took on the path toward the Cross?

Probably not. Francis would have cared only that he walked this path himself, regardless of how many steps it took. Francis's path wasn't measured in steps; it was measured in exemplary living and faithfully showing the kindness of Christ to all.

I walked a lot of steps in Assisi. I wonder if some of them actually fell on the same stones as Francis's. Who knows? Certainly, I have walked the path of his younger, spoiled days. My feet have certainly fallen on the path of confusion, the path that seems to have no purpose or direction. On my best days, I follow the path of attending to the poor and the sick—of teaching and showing kindness. I can only hope and pray, though, that on the normal days, I tread a path toward conversion, for conversion doesn't always happen in a single flash of insight. Conversion is a lifetime journey toward holiness. As one theologian says, "The true mark of holiness is the character of a life that gives to others, that extends beyond the narrow frontiers of itself, its own comfort and concerns—a life that furthers the humanizing process."[1]

Francis expanded the frontiers of his own life and the frontiers of the lepers he washed. He expanded the frontiers of Clare, his most beloved disciple. In the centuries after his death on October 3, 1226, Francis has expanded the frontiers of countless disciples. His example continues to call people to holiness of life. Francis probably would have said that although he hadn't reached true holiness, he was getting there. We may not reach true holiness, either, but we move toward it. We practice this movement. We practice conversion. We practice orienting our lives away from destruction and chaos and toward wholeness and peace. Every day we are converted as we practice the steady, ongoing movement away from perfection and toward transformation of spirit and self. Conversion isn't a onetime event, as some may think. It is a way of practicing life, moving from one holy place to another—from here to God only knows where—step by step by step.

1. Spoto, *Reluctant Saint*, 213.

8

When's Lunch?

The Holy Land

THE HOLY LAND IS a crazy place. Think about all the images from Sunday school: peaceful pastures, quiet dirt paths, fields of sheep and lambs tended by handsome, well-groomed shepherds. Bring to mind all your felt-butterfly, bulletin-board, coloring-book images from Sunday school and throw them out the window, because that's not what it looks like. It's like New York City on steroids, except you can't understand the language.

Still, there's a raw beauty to it. The Old City of Jerusalem remains a bustling place of business and activity. It is littered with garbage, but you can still catch glimpses of the place where Jesus and his contemporaries might have walked. One morning, my tour group walked the Via Dolorosa, which is the path Jesus took as he traveled to Calvary, the place of his Crucifixion. This two-thousand-foot path winds throughout the city and is walked by pilgrims from all over the world, now as in centuries past. It is customary for groups or individuals to carry with them an actual cross as they walk. Following suit, our group had a cross. It could be carried easily by anyone, but it was just large enough to need careful attention. We took turns carrying a symbol that marked us as participants in this journey through time and space.

I must admit, I didn't have much room for the cross that morning, because I was already carrying a goodly amount of negativity and cynicism. It was 8:00 a.m. I was tired and in a bad mood. Traveling with such a large group of "pilgrims" had worn thin my otherwise compassionate and buoyant sprit. Surely, in this chaotic context, the Stations of the Cross couldn't—wouldn't—speak to my spirit. I was having an internal temper tantrum and needed some space. God, I'm going to take a pass on this one. When's lunch?

As we began to move, though, I tried to get a grip. I dropped my negativity and took on a beginner's mind. In meditation, a "beginner's mind" helps us approach each experience as if it is occurring for the first time. A beginner's mind helps us to be curious about each moment. Even if we've performed a particular action dozens, hundreds, or thousands of times, we can bring a new perspective to it. We can be more aware of how we brush our teeth or drink our tea. We can eat lunch with profound appreciation and mental clarity. When we bring a beginner's mind to an activity, we are open to what we have to learn from the experience. A beginner's mind helps us approach even the commonplace with a new set of eyes, setting aside the baggage we bring to it and the expectations we place upon it. Clearly, I had plenty of baggage, and I was taking it into this modern-day holy journey. So, I drew a few deep breaths and reentered the experience.

From place to place we roamed. We took turns carrying a wooden cross about three feet tall. We also took turns reading the scripture appropriate for each station.

Station One: Jesus Is Condemned to Death

By the way, the Stations of the Cross (also called the Via Dolorosa, or Way of Suffering) is a liturgy, or ritual, performed on Fridays, particularly during Holy Week—the week before Easter. Each of the fourteen stations, or stopping points, recalls a significant event in the passage of Jesus through the crowded streets of Jerusalem. Early in the life of the Christian movement, pilgrims would actually travel to Jerusalem during Holy Week to walk this path. As

Christianity spread, though, people couldn't always make the journey to Jerusalem. So, individuals and churches created stations they could walk locally.

Station Two: Jesus Carries His Cross

While we moved as a group, some of the locals gave us space. They knew that what we were doing was intended to be prayerful and careful, so they let us pass unobstructed. The majority of the time, though, we were just a large group of people navigating a typical morning rush hour. I'm sure most of the population had grown accustomed to seeing Christian tour groups in their crowded streets. "Get out of the way!" they must have thought. "We have work to do!" Another day, another crucifixion.

Station Three: Jesus Falls for the First Time

One of my former parishioners, David Crean, wrote a service for the Stations of the Cross. I remember a line from his liturgy: "It's easy to fall in Jerusalem." No kidding. There are steps and tiny ramps everywhere. The streets are narrow. The stones are slick. As we walked, there were constant interruptions. Small tractors were bringing the morning's stock to vendors. They didn't slow down unless it was absolutely necessary. Men and women called us into their shops. Small children with huge backpacks were scrambling to school. Women sat along the walls selling grapes, figs, and herbs. The members of my group had varying degrees of pedestrian stability, shall we say. I spent a lot of time holding my breath, concerned that someone might trip, fall, and break a bone.

Station Four: Jesus Meets His Mother

At this particular station, the cross carrier and the reader of scripture happened to be a mother–daughter team. Anne, the mother, is a beautiful woman in her late sixties. Margaret, her daughter, is in her early thirties, a mother of two. As Anne held the cross higher than any other person had done, Margaret read from Luke's Gospel: "And the child's father and mother were amazed at what was being said about [Jesus]. Then Simeon blessed them and said to his mother Mary, 'This child is destined for the falling and the rising of many in Israel, and to be a sign that will be opposed so that the inner thoughts of many will be revealed—and a sword will pierce your own soul too.'"[1]

After Jesus was born, Mary and Joseph took him to the Temple to present him to the priest. This was a standard practice of the time. Simeon had been waiting for this moment all his life—the opportunity to see the Savior of the world. Simeon knew his greatness would come at a great price. He also knew Mary would be a witness to the great suffering of her son, which is why he told her a sword would pierce her soul.

Margaret read these words beautifully, and Ann continued to hold the cross high. The words took on a new significance for all of us. We knew Anne had lost her husband to a terrible battle with cancer exactly one year ago. We also knew that soon thereafter, her daughter, Margaret, called and asked if multiple sclerosis ran in the family. She was soon diagnosed with an aggressive form of MS. A former track star, Margaret did a great job of navigating the unsteady roads of Jerusalem, but she also knew when she needed to reach out for a hand to help her find her balance. As I watched Anne hold her cross high, I knew her heart had been pierced more than once. This is the price of loving someone deeply, of caring, of raising a child. I admired the bravery of Anne, this modern-day Mary, and tried to absorb, in some small way, the piercing of her heart.

When the readings for that station were over, Anne handed the cross to someone else, and we continued our journey, caring for the other, making sure we didn't fall, or trip, or lose our balance. Jesus fell several times in Jerusalem. We didn't want to.

The Stations of the Cross came alive in a very different way for me that morning. We were a small group of humanity walking

1. Luke 2:33–35 (NRSV).

through these ancient roads. We tripped, we doubted, we got hot, we complained, and some of us even fell a few times. We carried difficult realities in our hearts. We carried the bumps and bruises of life, looking for a blessing. We did all the things other wandering groups have done while trying to find hope. As we came to know and love Anne and Margaret, we shared the piercing of their hearts. We all wanted to take that burdensome cross from them, but we couldn't. All we could do was marvel at their bravery and their faith. I had never before experienced such an instantaneous moment of grace.

"When's lunch?" I had asked earlier. Boy, did I wish I could take that back. But I couldn't. It was just a part of the liturgy that revealed itself to me that morning. Mercifully, it gave way to yet another example of how God can turn our self-centered bullshit into something deep and expansive. I was reminded that the incarnational nature of God means that no matter what paths we walk and no matter what city we walk them in, Jesus has been there—is there.

A beginner's mind—a different way of inviting us to be more curious about God's movement in the world. It takes practice. It's not always easy to push through our old patterns and expectations, but God is always looking for ways to show us something new, even if it's a different way of seeing the same thing. I had awakened with a bad attitude, but by lunchtime, I had seen God and Jesus—a parent and a child. They were made real for me in the beautiful strength of Anne and Margaret, a mother and daughter walking bravely through the streets of Jerusalem.

May the Lord bless and keep them.

9

Ruined

I'M PRONE TO RUINOUS thinking. I come by it honestly. My mother has a habit of thinking she's ruined everything. "Well," she'd often say when I was a child, "that's certainly ruined now." "Don't ruin that!" she'd tell me, as if I were handling the delicate flakiness of precious gold leaf. There was no gold leaf in our home. Of a cake she was baking, or a squash casserole she had set on the counter, she would, without reason, declare, "It's ruined." Even today, my mother seems to take great pleasure in declaring something damaged beyond repair.

My sabbatical was not without moments of ruin. Sabbatical, a period of rest, takes its meaning from the word *Sabbath*. It is a chance for priests to get away, gain perspective, and experience renewal. This is a gift not many people are offered. But I was offered it, and for more than a year I planned, budgeted, and prepared my community for this period of time, during which I would take the phone off the hook and unplug. I would suspend my pastoral as well as my administrative responsibilities. I would do things that allowed me to catch my breath, expand my thinking, and reconnect with the ways God has called me to be me.

I, of course, worried constantly that I would ruin it.

"Oh no," I moaned to Matthew, "there's no air conditioning." In a lovely condo with a pool overlooking the Pacific Ocean, I was focused on the lack of air conditioning. "This is ruined," I said.

"Oh no!" I said to Matthew with a dramatic lilt. "There's no fan in this bedroom." In a lovely bedroom overlooking the old city of Assisi, where jolly men and chubby nuns greet each other every morning with a *buon giorno*, I was concerned that there was no fan. "The whole thing is ruined!" I thought.

Truly, these thoughts entered my mind and, more harmfully, entered into one of the most precious opportunities I have ever been given.

Meditation teaches us that nothing is solid. In my mother's world, by contrast, all things were solid. Everything that is solid can be destroyed, shattered, collapsed. When we think all things are solid, including our thoughts and experiences, we very naturally fall into the habit of thinking that certain moments of our life can be ruined. More disastrously, we can be seduced by the false belief that *we* have the capacity to ruin them. That we could ruin a moment—what a great amount of pressure this places on us.

If, as meditation teaches us, nothing is solid, then the positive side of the coin is that everything is fluid, or impermanent. This is a very anti-American way of thinking. Take Christmas. We prepare for it earlier and earlier every year. Commercials tell us that no other time of the year is more wonderful than Christmas. We should certainly make the best of it, right? We better do our best to make it spectacularly magical and wondrous and filled with love, gingerbread cookies, and sock-footed mornings with our favorite coffee. In other words, we'd better not fuck up Christmas!

I don't know about yours, but my Christmas mornings have never measured up to society's idealized image of the holiday. They were never as perfect as the Folgers commercials suggested they would be. My handsome brother never magically appeared on Christmas morning, safely home from the Peace Corps. Christmas came and went, and at 3:00 on Christmas afternoon, just so you wouldn't linger too long in a Christmas reverie, my father would declare, "Well, Christmas is over."

Yep, sure was. And, to prove it, my mother would already have fallen into her post-Christmas blues.

In meditation practice, there's a technique called "noting." Noting is the process of becoming aware of when we have been pulled from our focus on the breath or from any another object of focus. As I've said several times, meditation isn't about ridding the mind of distractions or thoughts, but about managing the distractions and thoughts that inevitably knock on our mind's door when we're trying to be still and quiet. Noting is a way of naming what is going on in our minds.

For example, when I'm meditating, I often experience a few seconds, a few breaths, when I am present and mindful. But then, before I know it, my mind has become unmoored. It has drifted toward what I had for dinner last night. "What an interesting thing Matthew made. I didn't know he knew how make Haitian dishes. Was that coconut milk? Wow, I remember going to Haiti. That was a difficult trip, but the people are so beautiful and kind. Did I ever send that e-mail asking Kim if I registered for the convention? When was the last time I jumped on a trampoline?" And so forth and so on. Clearly, I have lost my focus, so I make a mental note: "Thinking." The noting technique allows me to acknowledge that the mind has drifted, that it has begun to think. So, without judgment, I bring it back to the anchor of the breath. In and out. I start again.

The "without judgment" aspect of noting is the hardest part. My teacher says that we should note nonjudgmentally. The voice with which we note should be neutral, gentle. It shouldn't have an exclamation mark after it (Thinking!). It shouldn't be self-deprecating (Thinking, stupid!). We gently name our distractions and come back to the breath.

Distractions are an integral part of our practice. They teach us to move back and forth with flexibility and kindness. They help our spirits and minds become malleable so that they can bend with the changing circumstances of life. "Oh, I'm thinking again. No biggie. Nothing is ruined."

Clearly, bouncing back is not a strong point of mine, but the noting technique models how we can move through life with the assurance that we can navigate its detours productively. As the mind can drift, so can the spirit and body. The trick is to know that we've lost focus and that we have the skill and awareness to recalibrate. This takes practice, as most of us weren't raised to have this sort of mental resilience. I grew up believing that if one thing goes wrong, I may as well quit. If I have mismanaged, misspoken, misspent, misplanned, missed the mark, or missed anything at all, I am finished. "No air conditioning? We may as well leave now."

Meditation saved my sabbatical because it taught me that I can drift into irrationality and drift right back. No harm done.

Ahimsa—do no harm. I don't have to beat myself up if I do something wrong. All is not lost if I make a mistake. I do not have to lash out at others if I become fearful that my life is not perfect. Gray areas are a perfectly acceptable part of life.

There is a woman in my church named Nancy Rayfield. She is ninety years old. Nancy is a model of faithfulness and devotion. She loves her church, she loves her community, and she loves the arts. The most fabulous thing about Nancy, though, is her flexibility. You'd think that a woman aged ninety would be set in her ways. She's not. I think it has very much to do with her socks. Nancy's socks never match.

Very early in her life as a wife and a mother of three boys, Nancy decided that she would never again sort socks. "I never saw the point," Nancy told me. She said she kept a box on the top floor of their house. When she folded laundry, she'd just drop the socks into the box. When her husband or sons needed socks, they'd simply stop by the box of socks and grab two, any two. "Do people ever notice?" I asked. "I'm sure they do. But it's just one of those things about life I didn't want to worry about." What a great gift she gave to her family. One less thing to worry about. One more thing about which to be flexible and playful. Were her kids ruined by this experience? No. Was her family ruined? No. In fact, it set up a pattern of flexibility that would follow them the rest of their lives. This practice helped them know that in life, you can break from deeply held patterns and nothing will fall apart.

If we experience events as solid, like matching socks, we are more prone to fear ruining them. But if we perceive them as liquid, if we hold them loosely and gently, we realize they are not ours to ruin or to make successful. We realize that nothing stays the same and that if a moment doesn't work out the way we had imagined, another one is lined up right behind it, waiting to take off in a direction we might not have anticipated. There is another mismatched pair of socks always waiting to be born.

There were times during my sabbatical that I went batshit crazy (no judgment) with worry. So I spent a lot of time meditating, giving myself space to depressurize the situation. I spent a lot of time noting that old habits were resurfacing, habits that put a lot of expectations on every single moment. As with Christmas, I had better not screw up this sabbatical. The reality was that I hadn't ruined my sabbatical but that I certainly would if I kept up this harmful way of thinking. And that's all it was—thinking about and reliving old stories. Duly noted. Afterward, Matthew and I would get a cappuccino, watch the pigeons, and go on with our afternoon and evening.

Meditation has given me a new, very important tool. I can bounce back. I can reenter where I left off. I can make Christmases look however I want them to look. My socks don't have to match. I spend much of my meditation time thinking and noting, but that's OK. Each time I note, I am being honest with myself, and opening up another opportunity to return to my breath and pick up where I left off.

Chill, brother—nothing is ruined.

10

Churchgoing

Attending church on Sundays during Sabbatical

TOM, A RETIRED EPISCOPAL priest, has been a very influential person in my life. He served as a priest for thirty years and had a particular gift for mentoring young priests. Tom was my rector (the priest term for "boss") after I was ordained. This is an important relationship for a young priest, as a lot of formation happens during these first years. Tom was a good mentor. And, twenty years into our relationship, he remains a good mentor. On a recent visit, the relaxed, retired Tom said, "I had forgotten how good it feels to go to church."

For priests, going to church is, let's face it, a job. Our call is to administer the sacraments, hear confessions, tend to the sick and dying, offer care to the lonely and lost, and remind the world of God's presence in every holy and unholy moment. Sunday morning is an opportunity for members of the Christian community to remind themselves of God's presence and importance in their lives. Sunday is our day to reacquaint ourselves with resurrection, to put ourselves together in preparation for the sheer unpredictability of another week. This means Sunday is a big day.

For me, Sunday involves a 5:30 a.m. alarm and dressing in the closet so I don't awaken my husband and disturb his Sabbath.

(Funny, huh? First thing every Sunday, I spend time "in the closet.") From there, I greet the groggy hipster employees at Starbucks and review my Sunday sermon. And then it begins—off to the first of three services of the morning. I will greet hundreds of people. Some of them will expect me to know the intimate details of their lives (How was your visit with your granddaughter? Did you hear from your doctor?). Some will want my full attention (Father, do you have time for me to update you on my grandson's journey toward becoming a brain surgeon? It won't take but a minute). Some will avoid me because they're ashamed of their attendance record (I'm sorry, I haven't been to church in three weeks! I've been sooo busy). Others have suggestions (Father, do you have a few moments in which I can tell you a few things that need improving around here?). Some would like to gripe (Father, can I take a few moments to share with you the ways in which you and the Church have ruined my life?).

The three Sunday-morning services utilize as many as thirty volunteers, who will read the lessons, serve as acolytes, administer the chalice, teach our children, or greet people as they enter the sanctuary. Some of those people will show up. Some of them will not. Some will know what they're doing. Some will not. Filling gaps and giving instructions for tasks can make for a hectic morning, especially if volunteers show up two minutes before the opening bell. Sunday morning reminds me of getting ready for the opening night of a play—but it's an opening night that happens every week.

Needless to say, when the alarm rings at 5:30, I don't spring out of bed. I don't know what the day will hold for me, and I don't always look forward to "making Sabbath" for some three hundred people. So, when Tom told me he'd missed going to church, his words fell on hardened ears.

When I started my sabbatical, I was uncertain about whether I would attend church. Church has always been an important part of my week. I went weekly with my father to a very sweet, simple church in Speed, North Carolina. Later, in college, I found a larger, creative church. Dressed in a tie on Sunday mornings, I would trip my way across passed-out fraternity brothers and tiptoe around beer bottles and piles of vomit on my way out the door. I would return about the time they were picking themselves up. "Where have you been?" they'd ask.

Many priests, including me, get burned out on church. On vacations, we'll "take Sunday off." Ultimately, visiting other churches frustrates us, because they typically don't do things the way we would. Priests like me get frustrated when the churches we attend are wealthier, more successful, or better organized than our own. Also, I run the risk of working, scoping out things I might "borrow."

Truth be told, I was somewhat scared to attend church while on sabbatical. I was concerned that it would pull me back into unhealthy, un-Sabbath-like patterns. But the wise voice of my husband brought me back to myself.

"I think it's bullshit that priests get to take a break from church on Sunday," he said in his most forthright, and annoying, tone. There it was, out on the table. Church would be a part of my sabbatical. What follows is an honest record of where I went to church (or not) during my three-month sabbatical and what I remember.

Sunday 1 of 12

I didn't go to church. I didn't even consider it. Nope. No way.

Sunday 2 of 12

I thought about going to church, but didn't. We hadn't put any effort into finding a church in the area and were still trying to figure out Uber.

Sunday 3 of 12

SoCal

The church I attended in southern California was a very nice, modern church with sunlight flowing in. There was an instructed Eucharist. This is something priests do every now and then to educate the congregation about the church service, or liturgy. At various points during the service, the priest will stop and say, "We're doing this or saying this or singing this because . . ." I find instructed Eucharists annoying. I know, I know—they are helpful. But they turn the service into a classroom, and classrooms make me restless and give me a headache. I must concede, though, that this priest did a great job. Her instructions struck a good balance between the practical and pastoral. She was gentle and humble and had a good sense of humor. She made me consider the possibility of doing an instructed Eucharist in my own church. If I do, I will ask for her notes.

Their musician was a pianist. With every verse, he got slower and slower. By the fifth verse of "Amazing Grace," I wanted to shoot myself. This was not their permanent musician, so I reserved judgment (kind of).

That particular Sunday, the church was host to a blood drive. A blood mobile awaited willing donors in the parking lot. The message "give me your blood after church" might be a bit off-putting to a visitor, but I appreciated this church's message of stewardship— we give, or sacrifice, so that others can know life—a good message for Sunday, I think.

Sunday 4 of 12

Self-Realization Fellowship

Our favorite coffee shop was wedged between a yoga studio and the Self-Realization Fellowship, or SRF. The SRF was founded by Paramahansa Yogananda. In the small city of Encinitas, it has at least five locations, including a lovely oceanside meditation garden, which I frequented. Happening upon the SRF was definitely a surprise. I didn't seek it out, but it was up my alley and in line with my core beliefs as a religious person.

For more than eighty-five years, Self-Realization Fellowship (SRF) has been dedicated to carrying on the spiritual and humanitarian work of its founder, Paramahansa Yogananda, widely revered as the father of Yoga in the West.

SRF is a worldwide religious organization with international headquarters in Los Angeles. As expressed in the Aims and Ideals formulated by Paramahansa Yogananda, the society seeks, among other things, "To overcome evil by good, sorrow by joy, cruelty by kindness, ignorance by wisdom."[1]

I have been a practitioner of yoga since 1999 and have long believed in the ideals and value of aligning the body with the breath. I have been a practitioner of meditation since 2012 and firmly believe it leads us to a more profound connection with God through knowing and exploring ourselves more fully. Meditation creates a space that can be filled with God's love, compassion, and call to right action. Even though I'm totally on board with the guiding principles of the SRF, I approached it with cynicism. As a dude raised in mainline Christianity, cynicism is my go-to response to those who call themselves "spiritual, but not religious." I have become distrustful of this phrase.

Hence, my Christian tendency was to enter the SRF gathering with cynicism and, I admit, arrogance. But the service was no different from most Christian gatherings. We honored our teachers (which included Jesus). We discussed the power of meditation and how it brings about a deeper connection with the divine. We talked about how it benefits all religions to be in discussion and concord with each other.

What do I remember most? There was a very kind, cooperative, and welcoming spirit in the room, which, I must admit, felt a bit like the gathering space in a funeral home. Architecturally, I think this was a nod to the Christians in the house. Christians like their church to feel like church, or a funeral home.

1 Yogananda, "Aims and Ideals," line 8.

There was an attempt by the leader to discuss readings from all major religions. He did a good job of tying them together. He pointed to how each religion or expression of spirituality is about manifesting God's love and being kind to each other and to the planet.

During prayer time, we extended our hands and chanted *om*, a universal sound of harmony. We directed our intentions to the suffering, the sick, and the lonely. This act was very powerful for me. I wondered how we might do this in my own Episcopal congregation.

At the time of the offertory (the collection of gifts), we were instructed to hold our donation of money in our left hand and say the following prayer: "God, all that we have comes from you, yet we love you more than our things, so we give a portion of what we have to you that the world might be healthier." This was a powerful thing to do—to hold what we were going to give and name it as a small portion of what we give back to God for the doing of God's work. It made me think to myself, "Is this important? Is this all I can do?"

At the gathering of the SRF, there was no Holy Communion (bread and wine), and I missed it. This part of the Episcopal service has always reminded me of God's closeness and the intimacy God desires to share with her people. But even without this element, I did come away feeling like I had learned something about God, myself, and my fellow human beings. I felt like I was a part of a larger human family. I also forced myself to admit that although "spiritual" people aren't lame, they do need to cut us "religious" people some slack. We're all on the same team.

At first, I felt like I was betraying God by going to the SRF, but I did not betray God, because God was present. I don't think I'd like to go every Sunday, but going every once in a while would be a healthy part of a spiritual life and would help us all. In my opinion, it was a genuine expression of Christlike compassion.

Sunday 5 of 12

We flew to Italy. Since we were transitioning to Italy time and I was at my absolute grumpiest, I didn't go to church.

Sunday 6 of 12

Anglican Church in Assisi

Does the name Hyacinth Bucket ring a bell? She's a character on the British sitcom *Keeping Up Appearances*. Convinced she is of a higher pedigree than is actually the case, she therefore requires that her last name be pronounced *Bouquet*. She is often in the middle of others' business, whether they want her input or not. When we walked into the Anglican Congregation of Assisi, a tiny Christian community in the old city of Assisi, Italy, a woman very similar in appearance to Hyacinth was standing at the piano. She was loudly singing hymns while another woman sat at the piano and banged out the melody with her right index finger. Usually, a pianist helps the singer learn a tune. In this case, the singer—Mrs. Bouquet—was "assisting" the pianist in learning a few not-so-familiar Anglican hymns. "Oh God," I thought. "Here I am in the most religious place on the frigging planet—the place wherein the most sublime sacred music is authentically produced—and I've walked into a British comedy currently featuring a parody of the small-church experience." I didn't quite know what to do. Was this a prelude to a horrible service?

A congregation of fifteen was scattered across the small sanctuary. "I'm not going to be able to handle this," I told Matthew. I was looking for a way to bolt out the door without appearing rude. As I began to fake a cough and move to the nearest exit, the older woman at the piano turned and shouted to the room, "Does anyone here know how to play the piano?"

"He does!" shouted Matthew, who looked at me with a "got-cha!" expression on his face.

Matthew often accuses me of being a music snob. He's right, I guess. I want music to be done well, no matter what kind it is. Music is a window through which I can lose myself—a way I can glimpse eternity. Music is a path that leads me to the beauty and mystery of the burning-bush kind of God. I realize, though, that not all churches have the means to create this type of experience through music. My current setting was a stark reminder of this reality. Luckily, I knew most of the hymns that Sunday, and the hospitality of the congregation was warm. They were appreciative of what I had to offer. During the announcements, the vicar offered his thanks: "We are thankful to a person named Charlie, who is playing our hymns for us today."

What did I learn? When I'm attending another church, I try to hide the fact that I am a priest and to conceal my talents as a musician. But I'd like to believe that even if Matthew hadn't thrown me under the bus, I would have raised my hand. "Always offer your gifts," my friend and mentor always says. So I did. I was coerced, but I enjoyed playing for this congregation of the faithful and embracing the fact that I still have creative gifts to offer. More importantly, I was glad to be reminded that many congregations are in need of these skills; church musicians for this type of congregation are a dying breed.

At the keyboard, I had another beautiful moment. One of the hymns assigned for that day was "Stand Up, Stand Up for Jesus." It's not in our current Episcopal hymnal, but I played it often when I was a young church musician. Here in Assisi, of all places, I was able to remember my small congregation in Speed, North Carolina, which was often without musical (and clerical) leadership. Musical snobbery wasn't a part of my life then, thank goodness. Instead, my early church experience was about the learning of faith—the faith of my father and of the handful of other people who drove to that small church each Sunday morning. Here I was, playing a hymn I hadn't played in thirty-five years, reminded of another congregation three thousand miles away. It wouldn't be Sunday morning for them until seven hours from now, but my prayers went to them, and to the faithful community who sustained my farmer father and shaped his children.

I hoped this particular Sunday was an isolated incident—perhaps the organist was away on vacation or the church was searching for a new musician. But maybe this was their way of doing things—pulling a musician, for better or worse, from the congregation. I'm not sure, but at this church, some pleasant buttons were pressed for me. I was reminded that there are different ways of reaching the burning-bush kind of God. Maybe it's not through musical perfection. In the case of this congregation, it might be through the abundant meal they share at the Italian restaurant across the street. It might be how they come together, a small family, in one of the most sacred cities on the globe to pray, partake of the sacraments, and, with a small but mighty voice, sing of God's goodness and mercy.

Sunday 7 of 12

Church of the Samaritan

While in Jerusalem, we spent one Sunday in Samaria. Samaria is home to the Samaritans, as in the parable of the Good Samaritan. This is a story Jesus tells about a man who was beaten on the side of the road by robbers and left there to die. Several people passed the beaten man on the road: a priest, a Levite, and finally, a Samaritan. The Samaritan was the only one who stopped to attend to the helpless, wounded man. The Samaritan poured healing ointments on him, bandaged him up, and put him on his own donkey. He then took the man to a hotel and gave the innkeeper enough money to take care of him. "Look after him," the Samaritan said, "and when I return, I will repay you whatever more you spend."[2]

Jesus tells this story to demonstrate what it means to be a good neighbor. The twist is that in Jesus's day, Samaritans weren't considered neighbors. There was ancient bad blood between the Samaritans and the Jews. So Jesus is really turning up the heat

2. Luke 10:35 (NRSV).

when he tells his audience, experts in Jewish law, that yes, even the Samaritans are your neighbors. In fact, the story even delivers a blow to priests like me, the very people who did *not* stop to attend to this broken, beaten man on the side of the road.

So there we were, in Samaria itself, listening to the parable of the Good Samaritan. How surreal. After the service, we enjoyed a brief reception at which we greeted people and drank strong, spiced coffee. Afterward, the group traveled up and up and up, to the top of Mount Gerizim, where we visited a village of actual Samaritans. Some eight hundred Samaritans have lived in this small mountain village for 3,654 years. The day of our visit was on September 13, their New Year's Day. We met the high priest, who can trace his lineage all the way back to Adam in less than two hundred generations (we saw the family tree!). From there, we traveled to Jericho, the oldest city in the world, took a look at one of the few surviving sycamore trees in all of Israel (the tree that the height-challenged Zacchaeus climbed so he could get a glimpse of Jesus.)

I remember the priest of the parish saying we would never again hear this story without thinking about the day we were in ancient Samaria. He mentioned that we are all brothers and sisters, joined in the common goal of being kind to each other. Looking around at this small congregation, I thought, "Yes. Even this group of people who can't understand what I'm saying, who read their Arabic words from right to left, who drink insanely strong coffee, who live in a dry, difficult, place—I am neighbor to these people and they are neighbor to me."

"Who is our neighbor?" the lawyer asks Jesus in the story of the Good Samaritan. "I'm glad you asked," Jesus might have said, "because I've got a real doozy for you." Sometimes it's uncomfortable to be in the presence of our neighbor. I think Jesus was trying to say that in order to be a good neighbor—the kind of neighbor Jesus expects us to be—we have to empty ourselves. We have to rid our lives of ego and judgment. Being a neighbor involves being and feeling connected. This takes practice and vulnerability, whether it's with people who occupy a region six thousand miles away or the family across the street.

I remember a time when my denomination put a new emphasis on the part of our ritual called "passing the peace." About midway through the service, after we have confessed and are absolved of our sins, during that fleeting moment of spiritual purity, we are invited to share words of peace with our neighbor. Typically, we extend a hand to shake and say, "The peace of the Lord be with you." It's a beautiful gesture. But we Episcopalians don't like to touch each other. We like to keep to ourselves. On one occasion, a woman in front of me plunged her hands into her pockets at this point in the ritual. Her gesture of peace was a slight nod of her head. I'm not sure what she was afraid of, but she had resolved not to touch anyone in church, for God's sake. Eventually, the practice of passing the peace took. Episcopal churchgoers were seen hugging, smiling, and even moving out of their own pews, for God's sake! For God's sake. Yes, we pass the peace, we move out of our comfort zones for God's sake, and for the sake of peace. In Samaria, I was engaged in a global exchange of the peace with an ancient people. When I was twelve years old and learning how to pass the peace in confirmation class, I never anticipated that the idea of peace would become so real and fall so firmly within my grasp. As I shared God's peace with people who didn't know what I was saying, they had to trust the smile on my face and the touch of my hand.

I like to imagine that each Sunday, as I pass the peace with my congregation in Bloomington, Indiana, I'm doing so also with the good folks I met in Samaria, and even with *their* neighbors who are at war. Whether we do it in church, on the side of a road, or in line at the coffee shop, the sharing of peace is a practice. Based on what I read in the papers, we haven't gotten it right—not yet. Our neighbors still lie helpless, wounded, and overlooked on the side of life's roads. So, for God's sake and for the sake of all God's people, practice.

When you ask yourself seriously, and in the stillness of your heart, "Who is my neighbor?" you will realize how connected you are to every human heart. Meditating on this question will call you to humbly empty yourself so that God can sweep in and show you something or someone new and beautiful.

Sunday 8 of 12

Church of the Holy Sepulchre, Old City of Jerusalem

The Holy Sepulchre is the holiest of Christian sites. It marks the site of the tomb of Jesus—where he was placed when he was taken down from the Cross and from which he rose three days afterward. The tomb of Jesus lies within the large Church of the Holy Sepulchre. It's an incredibly complicated structure, with an even more complicated story behind it. I won't get into the details, but for now, let's just say the building is "shared" by many Christian denominations: Roman Catholic, Armenian Orthodox, Greek Orthodox, Egyptian Coptic Orthodox, Syriac Orthodox, and Ethiopian Orthodox Tewahedo. Within one building, they each have their own turf. I guess they missed the whole Christian thing about sharing, but I'm not in charge.

Thousands of tourists visit the site each day, and the day of our tour was no exception. The place was filled with pilgrims praying, kneeling, crying, kissing stones. There were lines to enter the other holy sites within the church, such as the place of the Crucifixion and the tomb of Adam. All the while, monks and priests were leading liturgies. Various processions weaved through the crowds. It was absolute chaos. "Be still and know that I am God," the psalmist says.[3] The psalmist never visited the Church of the Holy Sepulchre. And, to top it off, there was a line around the building to enter the tomb of the Resurrection. We'd try to see the tomb another day.

The second Sunday, early in the morning, Matthew and I walked back into the Holy City. The streets were quiet. The vendors had not yet opened their shops. We wandered into the Church of the Holy Sepulchre. There was a gentle hush to the whole place. You could hear priests chanting; the smell of incense was strong in

3. Ps 46:10 (NRSV).

the air. "Is the place closed?" I thought. No, it was open, and it was as if I had the whole place to myself.

I remember thinking, "Wow, I'm in the holiest place on earth on the holiest day of the week." I walked around slowly and absorbed the energy of the room. The various tenants were doing their thing. Franciscan monks were chanting. Orthodox priests were receiving disciples, who kissed their hands. A procession of Armenians came through, dressed in black, banging sticks on the floor. They disappeared into a room to begin their rituals. Candles were everywhere, left by pilgrims who might have needed prayers for their children or parents or lovers. And in the center, the tomb was empty.

The door of the tomb is about five feet tall. Since I'm 6'1," I bowed and went in. The inner chamber, lit only by candles, is the size of a small, rectangular closet. Immediately inside on the right, at knee height, is a stone slab, the place where Jesus was laid. A woman knelt over and rested her head on the slab, whispering her prayers as she rubbed the surface slowly with her palms.

If there was ever a place to pray perfectly, this was it. I panicked. I quickly realized I didn't know what to do in the presence of such holiness. Certainly, I couldn't be as holy as the woman next to me, who was giving everything she had to the experience. Her kisses and her tears were like those of the woman who washed Jesus's feet with expensive oil and wiped them clean with her hair. "What a lame priest I am," I thought.

We often don't know what to do in the presence of holiness. "What should I do?" I asked myself. I swallowed my pride and tried to be open to the moment. I followed suit and did what the woman was doing. I knelt, rested my head on the slab, closed my eyes, and felt the cool stone with my flat palms. I thought about all the people who had offered prayers in the chamber. I thought about Mary the mother of Jesus and Mary of Magdala, who had hovered around that place, crying, whispering, hoping. I thought about Joseph of Arimathea, whose tomb it might have been. He gave this tomb to Jesus. I imagined him placing his friend in it, quietly, gently. On this place where my head rested, the beaten, bruised, bloodied body of our Lord had lain. Why was I so worried about getting it right? In this place, God had acted. I don't know how, but in this place, God righted the imperfection of humanity. Certainly my imperfection would come as no big shock to anyone. I opened myself to the moment and realized that in this place, in every moment of every day, it was Easter.

So, I prayed. I prayed that Easter would always be alive in me and in my ministry.

How can you leave such a holy place? As an Episcopal priest, I am of the opinion that Easter happens everywhere, at all times. We take resurrection with us, and Jesus is always out there somewhere, resurrecting something. As I left the tomb and went back out into the morning light, I knew this would be my favorite moment, but a moment I couldn't hang on to. Meditation teaches us that, if we are to share, we must let go. We can't hang on to moments. They are not solid. Moments are liquid. As much as we'd like to hang on to a particular moment in time, we have to move on.

I think Jesus would agree that as holy as the tomb is, resurrection doesn't happen there anymore. The tomb reminds us of the power of God's love and God's ability to turn something horrible into something beautiful. Be we can't stay there. We have to go.

So, I left behind the beautiful, mysterious Church of the Holy Sepulchre. I may or may not see it again in my lifetime, but I take part of it with me into every Easter morning, into every Sunday morning, and into every moment.

Sunday 9 of 12

Calvary Episcopal Church, Tarboro, North Carolina

My mother lives in a retirement community called the Albemarle. It's in Tarboro, which is about eight miles south of our family farm, where I grew up. The closest Episcopal church, as I mentioned earlier, was in Speed—a tiny town. My father and I regularly attended this small church, which had a worship community of approximately twenty people. There was another church, though, that I had always known about, Calvary Church. "Calvary is a money church," my daddy used to tell me. It is located in historic downtown Tarboro, surrounded by a beautiful graveyard, which is enclosed by a brick wall. Calvary Church can hold about two hundred people, has lovely lanterns on each of the pews, and most importantly, has a real pipe organ. Once I was able to drive, I occasionally went to Calvary Church, mostly on Christmas Eve, and I eventually befriended their rector, Doug Remer. We developed a somewhat close relationship. I guess you could call him my first spiritual director and mentor. When Doug discovered I was taking organ lessons, he gave me the key and code to the church so I could practice on the pipe organ.

As I became older and more comfortable with the different "styles" of being an Episcopalian, I came to learn that, yes, compared to St. Mary's in Speed, Calvary Church was filled with mon-eyed people. It was and remains the epitome of the social church of the South.

On this tenth Sunday of my sabbatical, Matthew and I attended Calvary Episcopal Church. It was the first time I had taken Matthew to this sacred treasure. He'd heard about it for years. When I visit, I'm always a bit anxious about who will recognize me and want to talk to me. While I'm terrified that no one will recognize me, I am equally terrified of being recognized. It's strange. While I do not claim to be a prophet, going to church in your own hometown can be challenging.

The bell tolled and the service unfolded in typical fashion. The service was very nice. The preacher gave a decent sermon. The musician was good and led hymn singing well. The choir was small and gave it their best. On this particular Sunday, the community blessed needlepointed hassocks (cushions used for kneeling). The imagery on the kneelers was of local, North Carolina animals. Turkeys, raccoons, white-tailed deer, even opossums would accompany these worshippers on their journey of prayer and stillness. The needlepointed kneelers were charming and very well-done. I'd take the opossum home any day.

After the service, I was greeted by several people, some of whom knew me, and some of whom knew me but weren't quite sure how. "How, exactly, are you a Dupree?" a curious parishioner asked. "I'm the son of so and so," I said, and "I'm the brother of so and so." Now that I think about it, it's a very biblical way of identifying myself. "Charlie bar-Bubber," I might have said in biblical times (Charlie, son of Bubber).

Those who greeted us seemed super excited that I was a part of a gay couple. It was as though I were one of the scarcely seen, elusive animals on their newly stitched kneelers. I could almost hear them saying, "Look! A gay couple. We need one of those. Grab 'em!" Good for them. I applaud their enthusiasm and huntsman-like fervor.

I had arranged to meet a longtime family friend, Athlea Shelton, after the service. Since I didn't have grandfathers when I was growing up, I adopted one from our small congregation. Henry Gray Shelton sat three pews in front of us in church. He was a distinguished, faithful, gentleman farmer. One day, I decided I would invite him to be my grandfather, and he accepted. His wife, then, became my adopted grandmother. All my life, we would stay in touch with each other. Henry Gray died in 1988. All these years later, Mrs. Shelton, at ninety-seven, continues to be interested and involved in my life. She was the very last person I wanted to find out I was gay.

I feared she wouldn't understand. When Matthew and I announced our wedding, I went to great pains to keep all invitations, announcements, and mailings out of her zip code. (I don't know how I expected to keep her or her family from reading the *New York Times*—did I mention that Matthew and I were in the *New York Times*?) Needless to say, she found out. I received a note from her telling me how happy she was for both of us. "I've always wanted you to find someone," she wrote, "and I'm glad you have." Bless her dear, sweet heart.

In this case, I remember that the South continues to struggle with matters of human sexuality. I often forget that not all churches or their communities are "on board." The conversation continues among those who are fearful of how times are changing. I am thankful, though, that some are eager to include and welcome the LGBTQ community. And I am thankful for people like Athlea Shelton, who just want everyone to have an opportunity to find love.

Matthew met her for the first time on the day of our visit. She recounted to him the story of how our relationship began—in church. The Sheltons and I became an outside-the-box family that day in 1978, and Mrs. Shelton gladly welcomed Matthew into that family and into her heart. Like so many matriarchs before us, she sent us forward with her blessing, which means the world to me. I will always be thankful to her and to her family for welcoming me, and I will always have a special place in my heart for St. Mary's Church in Speed, North Carolina, the birthplace of this beautiful, loving, unconventional, incarnational relationship. I may not get to see Mrs. Shelton again, as she is very frail and bone thin. But I will forever remember that last visit with her.

She apologized for not having had time to fix her hair in time for our visit. It didn't matter to me.

"You're perfect," I said.

Sundays 10, 11, and 12 of 12

St. Paul's Episcopal Church, Beaufort, North Carolina

Beaufort is a little village near the coast of North Carolina. It is located on Beaufort Inlet, which leads to the Atlantic Ocean. It is almost completely surrounded by water and has a rich pirate lore and fishing history. It is the third-oldest town in North Carolina. This Beaufort (pronounced BOE-fort) is not to be confused with the Beaufort (pronounced BUE-fort) in South Carolina. The Episcopal church in the former is St. Paul's, the cornerstone of which was laid by the bishop of North Carolina on April 14, 1857. The church itself was built by shipbuilders. It is a beautiful church, and if you sit in the pews, you will have the distinct impression that they, too, were constructed by shipbuilders who built for stability, not comfort. It was in these pews that I spent my last three Sundays of sabbatical.

On the first Sunday I went to the early service, the one usually reserved for those who don't like music and prefer the Church's more traditional style of worship. I sat beside Tom, who in his early years as a priest was the rector of this very church. We offered our responses in the Elizabethan language of an era long gone—a tradition we in the Church have managed to hang on to. Here's one of my personal favorites:

> We acknowledge and bewail our manifold sins and wick-edness, which we from time to time most grievously have committed, by thought, word, and deed, against thy divine Majesty, provoking most justly thy wrath and indignation against us.[4]

You don't get to say that much anymore, now do you?

It was good to sit beside Tom in church again. I thought of the many hundreds of times we had sat beside each other while conducting church services, he preaching and I presiding over the liturgies. I remembered all the small things priests share with each other, things you'd never dream would take place between persons ordained for God's work: I'd help him find his reading glasses and hand him tissues when he sneezed; he'd tease me and tell me I looked like Niles Crane from the show *Frasier*. We'd gossip a bit, talking about who was in church that day, who was mad at whom, who was mad at us. I remembered him teaching me how and how not to do this or that. I remembered the arguments we had, one of which happened on a Christmas Eve when he was dressed like a shepherd, complete with headdress and crook—attached to his costume was a microphone that broadcast the entire argument to the congregation. I reflected on the necessary skill of the seasoned priest who mentors a young, cocky priest fresh out of seminary, who surely knows best. Tom was and is a good teacher. It was good to sit beside Tom on this day, on this side of the altar rail, and remember our journey together.

4. *Book of Common Prayer* (New York: Church, 1979), 331.

Of course, we couldn't help but offer some critique of the service: the sermon had a good point, but it was a bit long. Otherwise, the service was a good experience that made me feel like I had actually worshipped instead of just going through the motions. I was still hoping, though, that the fires of my churchgoing experience would once again be lit.

The second Sunday in Beaufort, I went to the late service with Matthew. At one time, there was a small pipe organ at St. Paul's. It had been replaced with a shorter, more compact electronic organ. I wondered why a pipe organ would be replaced. My sources told me that the taller pipe organ stood in the way of a stained glass window that had been given in honor of the window donor's mother. The shorter organ didn't block it. Still, the organ sounded lovely and led congregational singing well. The choir did a fine job. The choir director clearly knew how to choose music that is challenging and accessible (and appropriately brief). He played too quickly, though, and didn't allow me to catch my breath. The sermon had a good point. But, as Mr. Henry Gray Shelton used to say, "That preacher sure did miss some good stopping points."

I couldn't shake the feeling, though, that I had fallen out of the practice of going to church. My priest hat was still on, and I couldn't help being an interloper instead of a worshipper. I wasn't able to get into the spirit of being in God's house of prayer. I always tell people who are church shopping to attend the same church at least five Sundays in a row so they can get a sense of the community. I had a few opportunities left.

On my third Sunday, things began to feel more comfortable. I stopped critiquing, and the flow of the service seemed more prayerful. I was able to let go. Most importantly, the preacher was preaching a good sermon, and at just the right moment, I thought, "Please stop there. Please stop there." He did. The church's annual giving campaign also launched that day. As I listened to the speaker discuss the importance of giving, I believed him. Yes, we do need to give to our communities of faith. "At this time, the world needs the Church," he said. This was my *aha* moment. The world does indeed need the church at this moment in time. I had forgotten that the Church meets the need for community and closeness, that it offers the reminder that we are not the center of our respective universes. The Church is there to remind us to connect with others, to be aware of our connectedness to the planet, and to connect with ourselves. The Church is there to remind us of our breathing, not just the breathing of the present moment, but the breath that issued from God when God made us. And, as my friend Anne Jones likes to say, the world needs the Church because there must be a place to which we go to say "thank you" and "I'm sorry."

What did I learn from the reestablishment of this sacred, consistent pattern of communal worship? I learned that we can fall out of the practice of churchgoing. I see it all the time. A person gets deeply involved. They join everything. They get excited. They are involved regularly for six to eight months. Then, they miss once or twice—and then six or eight times. When I see them in the grocery store, they duck behind the Cokes. Every now and then, when I'm able to talk to these people, they sputter about how complicated life is, but I can tell. They simply stopped coming. They fell out of the practice.

Even I was tempted to simply not go, and I made up plenty of excuses for why I should just stay in my bathrobe and drink coffee. If the church community isn't accepting or friendly, why go to church? If the music is boring, why go to church? Why go if the ritual is cookie-cutter or the preacher preaches too long?

Because it's a practice.

As with every other worthwhile practice in our lives, we sometimes have to force ourselves into it. Sure, there are times when we think, "I'm really looking forward to my workout today." But most days, we have to forcibly put one step in front of the other to get to the gym. On the last Sunday of my sabbatical, I almost told Matthew, "I'm skipping today." But, for whatever reason, I did not. I went. I had become somewhat familiar with this community—familiar enough to look forward to the good they were doing, and familiar enough to put my personal preferences on the back burner. The important thing was that I remembered what it felt like to go to church. With what felt like warm water rushing through me, I remembered the feeling of being supported and sustained by this rhythm of listening, praying, singing, listening, looking, wondering, listening. I remembered what it felt like to be stirred to think about why, just why, all these other people came to church. I remembered getting involved in the stories of those receiving communion, wondering what was in their hearts. What hardships did they bring with them to the altar rail? I remembered wondering, as I watched very old people take the bread and the wine, how many times and through how many circumstances of life they had faithfully sipped from this tiny silver cup. I wondered what they had gone through that week, and what prayers hovered in their spirits. And, most importantly, I remembered wanting to be a part of this terribly important thing called the Church.

To this day, I still wonder, how important is the Church? I can't be certain. All I know is that when we are at our best, the Church is the best thing on earth. It is a place to embrace mystery, to let our minds wander, and to imagine that our personal goals aren't the most important concerns. It is the place where we come to practice being holy—where holiness is modeled for us by the faithful of our time and of times past. Church is the place to practice being better, being ourselves, being imperfect. Church is the place where we practice falling, getting picked up, and picking up others. Churchgoing takes practice—is a practice—just like any other thing worth doing. We aren't magically transported into the pews. But the lessons we learn there are an accumulation of lessons taught by mothers, fathers, shipbuilders, public-school teachers, nurses, saints, and scoundrels.

"I had forgotten how good it feels to go to church," Tom said.

Once again, Tom taught me an important lesson. Tom, the faithful, attended church. Not because he had to, but because it was his practice. I read all the time about yoga practitioners who leave their mats unrolled so they will be reminded to move into their asanas. I hear meditation practitioners talk all the time about how to prevent meditation from becoming automatic, stale, or unproductive. All practices have the potential to become dry and uninspiring. But in practicing, new windows are opened into who we are, who our neighbor is, and the quality of our relationship with the holiness and beauty of life.

As I concluded my sabbatical, I expressed gratitude for all the people who have shaped my life and influenced my ministry. I expressed thanks for Mother Church, who has structured my life and channeled my gifts and talents in productive and creative ways. And I expressed thanks to God, who, in a pew made by hearty shipbuilders in Beaufort, North Carolina, helped me to remember what I had forgotten: "Man, I want to be a priest one day."

11

Meditation, Interrupted

SHORTLY AFTER RETURNING FROM sabbatical, I had a morning appointment with my gastroenterologist. I arrived, as they had suggested, fifteen minutes early with my insurance information. At 8:30, I was taken back to the examination room, asked questions by the nurse, weighed, and given a blood-pressure test. Then—you know the drill—I waited. And I waited some more. Since it was so early, I hadn't been able to squeeze in my meditation practice. "Why not meditate here?" I thought. Hmm. But wouldn't that be strange? What if someone sees me?

"You're meditating? In a doctor's office? I'm calling the police!"

I decided this would be my object of focus: what is this fear all about?

I began with the typical preliminaries: breathing with my eyes open, closing my eyes, locating my breath in my body. To become aware of my surroundings, I snuck a peek: exam table, cotton balls, a plastic replica of the large and small intestines. I did a body scan with a special shout-out to my colon. I set an intention. Because I knew I'd be distracted, I included a few rounds of counting my breath. Then, I focused on what was zooming through my mind—paranoia.

I stayed with that feeling for quite a long time. I breathed space into the tense places in my body and mind. I lived with the question, What if I get caught? What will happen?

Isn't it funny how much we worry about looking stupid? We worry that people will see our weaknesses. If we need to meditate, the perception is that something's not right, right? We are comfortable going to the doctor's office, announcing to the world that our bodies are fragile, but we have a hard time quietly acknowledging that our minds need attention, too. They are fragile, overworked, and sensitive. How do we attend to their delicate circuits and ingrained tendencies? How do we redirect their fearful, destructive patterns?

Speaking of patterns, my thoughts returned to my need to be productive. I'm terrified that someone is going to catch me doing nothing. Why do nothing when you could be reading? There were plenty of magazines around. I could study up on irritable bowel syndrome or reacquaint myself with the nervous system. "Wait a minute," I thought. "If there's any place to attend to personal health and well-being, it's in the doctor's office, right? Nobody's going to embarrass me here."

Finally, I began to trust my surroundings. I trusted that even if the doctor thinks I'm a weirdo, he's not going to say anything about it. And, truth be told, I trusted that the doctor's soft, obligatory warning knock would give me time to regain my sense of presence and control.

Of course, on this particular visit, the doctor didn't knock.

He opened the door with the force of a Norwegian warrior. I jumped with such suddenness that he asked if I was OK. My eyes often water when they are closed. "I'm fine," I said, wiping my eyes. He stared at me for an awkward moment, then launched into his spiel, asking about my colon. Holy shit, was I embarrassed.

I find it particularly appropriate that on that day, the last to be recorded in this memoir, my meditation experience ended in utter embarrassment. It was not a perfect experience. My meditation teacher, however, would say that it was. She would say that the doctor bursting in on my meditation session was perfect—exactly the medicine I needed.

And maybe she would be right. It was just another example of how we can't hold on to or control experiences, the exciting ones or the embarrassing ones. We have to practice letting them go. For sixteen years, I have been blessed with being a priest—the handler of holy things. I have baptized children, blessed the dying, prayed with those who are sick and suffering. I have worked with the homeless and the hungry. I have talked people through anxiety attacks in the middle of the night. I have been with a mother and father as they spent final days and nights with their child in hospice care. I doubt I did any of these things perfectly.

"You don't have to be perfect," members of my congregation often say. "Sure," I think to myself, "that's what you think. But just wait until I am not perfect for you."

Herein lies the trap. Can I be perfect for everyone, or even anyone? Hell to the no. So what do we do?

We stop fearing our imperfection. We become comfortable and familiar with it. We draw upon the wisdom of the ancient teachers who tell us we are "but dust."[1] We embrace our impermanence and the fluid nature of life. We stop trying to nail everything down; we stop feeding our desire to be right all the time and to appear in control all the time. We accept that when we get things wrong or don't do things perfectly, the bottom won't drop out.

We are not alone in this fear. Our fears and imperfections connect us, in a very real way, to others. Meditating brings us to the blessed reality that none of us is perfect, no matter how hard we try to convince the world otherwise. Instead, each of us has a unique way of being imperfect, of being beautifully and wonderfully flawed, awkward, clumsy, insecure, and embarrassed.

Once we befriend these imperfections, they become gifts. Like the constellations that make up the complexity and wonder of the night sky, they tell us what we really are: holy, beautiful, and honest.

I've worked my whole life to be honest and real. I'm getting there. Meditation has allowed me to be gentler and more flexible.

1. Ps 103:14.

It has allowed me to roll with the punches, go with the flow, and generally speaking, bounce back from the troublesome situations that life and people inevitably present. We can rarely establish control over the difficulties that confront us. But we can control our reactions, and meditation has helped me do just that. There is now more space between the action and the reaction. I am less judgmental, even of those who tend to make life difficult.

Authentic involvement in life requires courage. And courage can push our buttons. It can take us to places that are ugly and beautiful. Meditation can help us focus on the beautiful—even when the beautiful is tragic and sad and necessary.

Dare to be still with your thoughts. Dare to be imperfect.

The way I read the stories of the Bible, God has a special love for our imperfections. God has a pattern of taking those covered-up parts of our lives and turning them into something amazing. God is doing the same thing with you.

May you, and all of your imperfections, be a blessing.
May your practice bring you freedom from that which is not serving you.
And to this warring world, may your practice bring peace.
Shalom. Namaste. Amen.

Postscript

I HIGHLY RECOMMEND SABBATICALS. They are quite the blessing. If you are lucky enough to have the time to get away, or seek the opportunity to reconnect with yourself, I am open to a conversation with you. I will help you think through timelines, details, intentions, and budgets. Most importantly, I will offer a clear reminder that this sabbatical is about you. You will want to make it about other people. You may feel the urge to make your sabbatical about your kids or your family or your church community. But I will remind you that this time is about the you of right now. I will remind you that this time is about God's desire for you and that this desire is not selfish. I will also encourage you, during this time, to meditate. For however long you're there, or wherever you go, you can start a journey of the mind and give yourself, and this world, a modicum of stillness, calm, and clarity.

Bibliography

Book of Common Prayer. New York: Church, 1979.

Martin, James. *Becoming Who You Are: Insights on the True Self from Thomas Merton and Other Saints*. Mahwah, NJ: Paulist, 2006.

Spoto, Donald. *Reluctant Saint: The Life of Francis of Assisi*. New York: Penguin, 2002.

Stoffregen, Brian P. "Exegetical note on Luke 10:38–42." http://www.crossmarks.com/brian/luke10x38.htm.

Yogananda, Paramahansa. "Aims and Ideals." http://www.yogananda-srf.org/Aims_and_Ideals.aspx#.V-1s5snkqaQ